V-1 V-2

The full story of the year Hitler's guided missiles fell on London.
Only five minutes from launch to impact—not even enough time to sound an air raid alert. They could not be tracked and they traveled too high and too fast to be shot down. This is not a scenario of World War III, but the story of the development of the Nazis' secret weapons and the devastation they wrought that, given a little more time, might have turned the tide of World War II.

Seen through the eyes of the Germans who devised and launched these weapons, as well as the people on the receiving end, here is an unprecedented "you are there" reconstruction of those times when the death throes of the Nazi empire claimed tens of thousands of Allied civilian casualties.

By the same author:
THE LONDON BLITZ:
The City Ablaze

V-1

HITLER'S VENGEANCE
ON LONDON

V-2

DAVID JOHNSON

Scarborough House/*Publishers*

Scarborough House/*Publishers*
Chelsea, MI 48118

FIRST SCARBOROUGH HOUSE TRADE PAPERBACK EDITION 1991

V-1/V-2 was originally published in hardcover by
Stein & Day/*Publishers*

Cover design by Bart Morris

Library of Congress Cataloging-in-Publication Data

Johnson, David, 1950-
    V-1, V-2 : Hitler's vengeance on London / David Johnson.
      p.   cm.
    Includes index.
    ISBN 0-8128-8527-9
    1. London (England) – History – Bombardment, 1944-1945. 2. World
War, 1939-1945 – Aerial operations, German. 3. V-1 bomb. 4. V-2
rocket. I. Title.
D760.8.L7J639   1991
940.54′4943 – dc20
                                    90-23902
                                        CIP

Contents

List of Illustrations

List of maps and line illustrations

Acknowledgements

On an uncommonly sunny London afternoon, the kind of day that makes a person forget that war even exists, a man calmly describes how his shop was demolished by the blast of a pilotless Flying Bomb. In a New York office building on a cold and blustery February day, a woman visibly tightens up when she remembers a V-2 rocket's unexpected impact. An ex-GI gets down on his hands and knees and half crawls under the table of his Manhattan apartment to demonstrate how he took cover from an incoming 'doodlebug'.

Hundreds of books and periodicals and documents in several languages went into research for this book on London under the Flying Bomb and rocket attack. But it is the experiences and reactions of people like these three, on both sides of the Atlantic Ocean, that gave life to it.

I would like to thank the following publications for helping me to get in touch with so many eyewitnesses of the German Vengeance Weapons attack. In the United States:

The New York Times Book Review
Air Force Magazine

In London:

The Evening News
The City of London Recorder

So many people went out of their way to lend their assistance. Fireman Blackman of the London Fire Brigade made available some invaluable records of the National Fire Service in 1944-1945. Without those reports, research would have been a much more difficult job.

James O'Sullivan, also of the London Fire Brigade, once again very kindly offered his assistance and his knowledge of the Brigade's men and organisation, putting me in touch with many people at Fire Brigade Headquarters and coming up with several helpful suggestions. The best of health to him.

In the United States, Jack Blackham of El Paso, Texas, deserves a Thank You for running down the information concerning the mid-air destruction of a V-2 by machine-gun fire.

The Still Picture Branch of the National Archives in Washington, DC managed to dig out some of the best photos of the V-1s and V-2s that I have seen. Their co-operation and assistance is greatly appreciated.

At the Imperial War Museum in London, the entire staff of both the Department of Documents and the Department of Printed Books were as courteous and helpful as always. Once again, I would like to single out George Clout for a special vote of thanks. Just as he had done when I was researching my earlier book *The City Ablaze*, Mr Clout came up with any number of invaluable suggestions, pointing out records like the Air Ministry Intelligence Reports which would have been overlooked by me except for his thoughtfulness.

I used several wartime diaries in the writing of this account, and would like to thank the owners for granting permission to quote from these diaries:

Vivienne Hall, for her diary.

Joan Reid, for the wartime notes of her aunt, Hilda Neal.

Alex Mitchell, for Mrs Gwladys Cox's London War Diary.

Under the heading of 'Giving Credit Where Credit Is Due', I would like to say a large thanks to Peter Hammond and his charming bride Carolyn. Carolyn's assistance in the Chiswick Library's records department was a very great help in piecing together the Staveley Road V-2 incident; good librarians should be encouraged! Peter's photography is excellent, and is also hugely appreciated.

List of Contributors

Each of the persons listed below gave their own personal and unique views of this distinctive phase of the war. Not every name is mentioned in the book, nor is every story used – mainly because of repetition – but every letter and interview was taken into account when this book was being written. All were tremendously helpful and are immensely appreciated.

Robert J. Alexander: U.S. 8th Air Force
S. Allenson
Morley Ayearst: U.S. Embassy

George Berryman: U.S. Office of War Information
Jack Blackham: 34th Bomb Group, U.S. 8th Air Force
William F. Boni: Associated Press
Dennis Bosher: Chiswick, West London
Lothar H. Bossing: Wehrmacht
A.W. Bourne: Fulham, Central London
H. Bryant: Forest Gate, London
Lilian H. Buck
John Butt: Plaistow, East London

George Clifford: National Fire Service
Don Cumming: Yeoman First Class, U.S. Navy
Edwin Carter: T/5, H.Q. ETOUSA
John E. Connor: 404th F.B. Group
Joseph Connor: 669th Bomb Squadron (L)
P. Cook: Home Guard, Bromley, Kent
P. Channing: Canning Town, East London
Miss Florence Cherry: Holloway Road Tube Station
Mrs Vicky Cattle: Bethnal Green, East London

Dick Dudley: T. Sgt., U.S. Army
Barbara A. Dicks
E.L. Davilia: 2nd Lieutenant, U.S. 8th Air Force
Angelo Darrigo: 9th Air Force H.Q., Colchester, Essex
Rosalind Depas: Bromley, Kent
J. Day: Ealing, West London
Mrs B. Doyle: West Kensington, London
Leon Drucker: Cricklewood, London
Albert Dudmesh: Home Guard

John Edgar: Peckham Rye, London

Irene Fudge: Old Southgate, London
R.R. Fillery: Croydon, Surrey
R.E. Foster: Wandsworth, South London
Ron Fowler: Smithfield Market Incident

Elizabeth Grace: Dulwich, London
P.W. Green: Flight Sgt., R.A.F.
Adele A. Gaudin: St John's Wood, London
Mrs Gunn: Walthamstow, East London
James Goldsmith: Clacton-on-Sea, Essex
Mrs Arthur E. Green: London

Philip Haring: Aldwych Flying Bomb Incident
Paul F. Harris: U.S. Army Air Force
J.K. Havener: 344th Bomb Group
Betty Hinman
Dennis Horsford: St John's Wood, London
Andre Hurtgen: Shepherd's Bush, London
Margaret A. Hutcheson: American Red Cross
George L. Hyman: Sgt., U.S. Army Air Force

A.R. Idenden: City of London

William H. Johnson: Tottenham, North London

June Kear: W.R.N.S., Stanmore, Middlesex
Vick Knight: U.S. Armed Forces Network, London

Tarina Lewis: Holland Park, London
Gerard van Loon: U.S. Army, British War Office, London

Mrs Lotte Linder
Mrs Kitty Lewis; Bexleyheath, Kent
Leonard Lincoln: Smithfield Market Incident
Iris Longmoor: Croydon, Surrey

Jordan Y. Miller: U.S. Army
Gillian Moreby
Mrs M. Malden: City of London
Elizabeth McDougald: American Red Cross, London

Loelya Northeroff: Devonshire Street, London
Otto Neuchel: Flying Bomb Launch Unit, Pas de Calais and Holland

Frederick Offord: National Fire Service

Mrs W.A. Pavier: Highbury, London
Mrs E.L. Price: Highbury, London
Mrs Joan Page: Twickenham, Middlesex

Julian Roffman: 4th Canadian Armoured Division
Sumner Rodman: S.H.A.E.F.
Michael D. Rose: Upper Norwood, London

Reino P. Saare: U.S. Army, Kew, Surrey
Jill Shelly
Mrs E. Ship: South Kensington, London
Gillian Simmons: W.A.A.F.
Henry Slegers: Antwerp
Jay W. Smith: 1st Lieutenant, 391st Bomb Group
Truman Smith: 385th Bomb Group (H)
E.A. Soan: Bromley, Kent

Colleen Tracy: Wood Green, London
Richard L. Temple: Lt. Col., U.S. Army Air Force
Percy Waxer: L. Cpl., 1st Canadian Army
Ivy White: Herne Hill, London
Leroy C. Wilcox: U.S. 381st Bomb Group
Hans van Wouw Koeleman: The Hague, Netherlands

W. Young: Teddington, Middlesex

CHAPTER ONE

A Terrible Vengeance

A group of American GIs stood talking outside their hotel in the West End of London. On leave and looking for some entertainment, they calmly debated where they should go and what they should do for the rest of the day. The discussion buzzed back and forth for a few minutes, until one voice piped up loudly, carrying above all the others. 'No thanks!' the young soldier protested, 'I've done enough sightseeing. And besides, after you've seen one bomb ruin, you've seen 'em all.'

In the spring of 1944 there were plenty of bomb ruins to be seen. During the fifty-plus months since the war began, London had endured countless hours under fire and hundreds of air raids. The Blitz, the first battle of London, had lasted from September 1940 until May 1941, inflicting widespread damage throughout the city. While the tide of the war turned against Nazi Germany in the North African desert and the sky over Occupied Europe during 1942 and 1943, hit and run raids by the Luftwaffe livened up many a blacked-out night. From mid-January to mid-March 1944 came the 'Baby Blitz', all-night raids that once again sent Londoners to their air raid shelters.

Throughout London derelict houses disfigured the tidy suburban streets. Lack of paint had allowed dry rot to spread, giving even undamaged houses an unkempt appearance. An occasional bomb crater marked the place where a building once stood.

In some districts, whole blocks had disappeared in the bombing and were now just large, vacant fields. St Paul's Cathedral stood alone in the middle of a miniature meadow, surrounded by grasses and wild flowers – blue larkspur, red clover, purple toadflax – that replaced blitzed shops and office buildings.

These flowers were the few spots of colour in an otherwise drab and dreary city. An American sailor stationed in London somewhat romantically compared the capital to 'a very respectable charwoman, carrying on her onerous duties and waiting for better times ...'

Letters from native Londoners to friends in the country or overseas were rarely so poetic. They turn to the same phrases to describe the city: dim ... grey ... dark ... dirty ... grim ... old.

The weather wasn't helping at all to cheer things up. It had been abnormally cold and rainy throughout the spring, and the chill continued during the first days of June. But the climate was not the most talked about topic. Even more unusual than the weather had been the disappearance of the countless uniforms – Free French, Poles, Australians, Indians, and especially Americans – from London's streets.

Uniforms had been a common enough sight since the outbreak of the war in 1939, but during the past year the number of badges and caps and tunics of every style and cut reached the overflow mark. Soldiers, sailors, and airmen could be seen wandering about in any district of the city, sometimes singly, but usually in groups. In Central London, servicemen sometimes outnumbered the civilians. Now, suddenly, they were gone.

Correspondent A.P. Ryan of the BBC gives this impression of the strange absence of uniforms: 'London seems fuller than ever, but there are far, far fewer soldiers of all nationalities. I went to the theatre last night and it was packed. But there was hardly a uniform in the house. Americans, who were very thick on the ground, have now thinned out – not to the vanishing point, but getting on that way. Hotels, restaurants, cinemas fill up, but the audiences are mainly civilians.'

Everybody had their suspicions of where the soldiers had gone and why. In London and throughout southern England, people talked of little else.

At 9.33 on Tuesday, 6th June, their suspicions were confirmed. A radio announcement from General Dwight D. Eisenhower's head-quarters told the world that the long-awaited invasion of France had finally begun.

People can recall precisely where they were and what they were doing when they heard the dramatic D-Day bulletin, just as when war had been declared or, to Americans, when President Kennedy was shot. The most immediate reaction was relief mixed with anxiety. Strangers spoke to one another on the street, exchanging Invasion news or mentioning that they had a relative 'at the front'.

For several days afterwards, London devoured everything it could about the fighting in Normandy. Crowds peered at news placards and snapped up stacks of newspapers as fast as they came out. Yeoman First Class Don Cumming, the American sailor who compared London to 'a very respectable charwoman', recalls a crowd of people standing outside a radio repair shop, listening to a rebroadcast of the Eisenhower announcement. Yeoman Cumming also remembers queueing half an hour for a newspaper, which had a grand total of four pages.

By the week-end, it looked as though the invasion would hold. Allied armies were not making much of a push inland, but they were holding their ground.

Within a few days of D-Day, however, Prime Minister Winston Churchill delivered a sobering address, warning everyone not to become too euphoric. Churchill declared that it was a 'most serious time that we are entering upon', and emphasised that the hardest battles were still to come.

Churchill knew all too well what he was talking about. Reports from Military Intelligence and European underground organisations had informed him of strange doings in northern France, and at a small installation on the Baltic Sea called Peenemünde. He and his War Cabinet were well aware that German scientists and technicians had developed two long-range secret weapons, which would be launched against England. By June 1944 Churchill knew what the new weapons were, but did not know where or how soon they would be used.

The chiefs of the German armed forces did not know, either. Adolf Hitler himself did not know when the new wonder weapons would be launched, but he knew exactly where they would be aimed – London, the same target he had been trying to knock out since the summer of 1940.

Long before D-Day, the war had become a grim, losing struggle for

Hitler's Third Reich. The stunning victories of 1940, when the Luftwaffe and the armoured Panzer columns joined forces to overrun France and the Low Countries within a matter of weeks, were now nothing but a dim memory. Defeats in Russia and North Africa had destroyed the finest divisions of the German Army. The Wehrmacht, once the swiftest and most powerful of striking forces, had been stopped dead.

Within the Third Reich itself, cities and industrial centres were 'on the anvil' from combined Allied bomber forces. The US Army Air Force bombed them – Düsseldorf, Hamburg, Cologne, Berlin – in the daytime, and RAF Bomber Command attacked at night. Hundreds, sometimes over a thousand, Lancasters, Flying Fortresses and Liberators dropped hundreds of tons of high explosives. War production suffered and a heavy toll of civilian lives was taken. The bombing of Hamburg in July 1943 created a mammoth fire storm, which burned for days and left 50,000 dead. And the raids grew larger and heavier as D-Day approached.

Adolf Hitler and Luftwaffe *Reichsmarschall* Hermann Göring, who once boasted that no enemy bomb would ever fall on the Fatherland, dreamed of exacting a terrible vengeance for what the Allied air forces were doing to German cities. Hitler's desire to retaliate was especially violent. After the raid on Hamburg, he pounded the table and ranted on and on about smashing terror with counter-terror.

A few years before, Hitler and Göring would have ordered a series of massive air raids against London as a full measure of revenge. But the once supreme Luftwaffe was only a ghost of what it had been in 1940 and 1941. Losses in combat, and the switch to fighter production for defence, had drained away the strength of the bomber fleets. There would be no new Blitz forthcoming.

There were other ways, however. For a number of years, German engineers had been designing new methods of striking at the enemy. Two new weapons were developed: one was merely a pilotless jet-propelled aircraft; the other was a highly sophisticated long-range guided missile.

The people who built and tested these weapons gave them austere, drawing-board designations, but Propaganda Minister Josef Goebbels would change that. These new devices were claimed by the Reich and re-christened the Vengeance Weapons, *die Vergel-tungswaffen*, which would be known to the world as the V-1 and V-2. The jet-propelled airplane, the pilotless V-1 Flying Bomb, was expected to be ready for firing by late spring 1944. The V-2 rocket would not be ready until a few months afterward, by autumn, it was hoped.

Germany had begun its rocket programme as far back as the early 1930s, before Hitler came to power. The Army's Weapons' Department had taken a liking to rockets not only because they were new and revolutionary, but also because they were one method of getting around the hated Treaty of Versailles.

The Versailles Treaty, signed by the Allied powers at the end of the First World War, limited Germany to a very small army, reduced the size of the German navy, and prohibited submarines and warplanes. It made no mention of rockets, however. So in 1930 the Army began serious work on its missile programme.

As the director of its new rocket programme, the Army appointed a 35-year-old *Reichswehr* captain named Walter Dornberger. Dornberger's father, a pharmacist, wanted young Walter to be an architect. But when war broke out in 1914, Walter Dornberger, then a 19-year-old, enlisted in the army. By 1918 he had risen to the rank of lieutenant in the Artillery Corps. After the war, Dornberger was allowed to stay in the small *Reichswehr*, limited to 100,000 men by the Treaty of Versailles.

Dornberger was an engineer as well as an artillery officer; his new job as head of a still non-existent missile department appealed to him. By 1932 Captain Dornberger was hard at work on a rocket called simply *Aggregat 1* (a designation meaning 'prototype'), or *A-1*.

While at work on the *A-1* missile, Dornberger hired another man as an assistant, a young rocket enthusiast named Wernher von Braun. Wernher von Braun had been interested in rocketry and space exploration since childhood, and had been working with an amateur rocket society in Berlin. But in the 1930s Germany was plagued by depression and unemployment; von Braun's experiments in Berlin stopped because of lack of funds.

When Captain Dornberger asked von Braun to join him at the

Army Weapons Department at Kummersdorf, south of Berlin, the 22-year-old scientist jumped at the chance. At Kummersdorf, his rocket experiments would have the financial backing of the Army.

Between 1930 and 1932, the *A-1* was designed and built at Kummersdorf. It weighed about 330 lbs, but was not properly balanced and failed to fly. While Dornberger worked on ironing out the bugs on the *A-1*, Wernher von Braun, with an independent team, developed the *A-2*. A liquid-fuelled missile, stabilised by a gyro-mechanism, the *A-2* streaked to an altitude of 7,000 feet in December 1934.

Although the *A-2* was a success, it was nothing more than an experimental rocket, too small for military use. Next, work began on a larger, heavier model, the *A-3*. But Kummersdorf was too large a city for the testing of this new missile. A misfire might cause the missile to fall in a residential district, and might result in civilian deaths. Also, there would always be watchful, prying eyes keeping track of the rockets, looking at every move made at the test centre.

Adolf Hitler had gained control of the German government in 1933, and declared himself *Der Führer* of the Third Reich a year later. By Hitler's orders, all military efforts were to be carried out in the strictest of secrecy. Another site would have to be found for testing the rockets.

Wernher von Braun recalled that his mother used to mention an island just off the northern coast of Germany, in the Baltic Sea, named Usedom; her father used to hunt ducks there. The way his mother told it, Usedom sounded like the ideal place for guided missile tests – it was by a sea coast, and secluded.

Late in 1935 von Braun visited the island and found it perfect. It was densely wooded, sparsely populated, and the Baltic Sea offered a 300-mile-long range for test shots. When Walter Dornberger saw Usedom, he agreed with von Braun.

The Wehrmacht and the Luftwaffe jointly purchased the island's north-western peninsula in 1936. During the following year, sections of forests were cleared and buildings of every description began emerging from reams of blueprints – wind tunnels, test stands, power stations, workers' housing – all under strictest secrecy. All this activity took place near the former fishing village of Peenemünde.

While the Peenemünde base took shape, work on the rockets continued. The third experimental rocket, the *A-3*, was tested in 1936 and 1937, and a great deal was learned from this temperamental missile. By autumn 1939 the military rocket, called *A-4*, was on the drawing board, although still untested.

Adolf Hitler had never been terribly enthusiastic about rockets. His military advisors thought that the *A-4* was nothing but an exotic toy, requiring a lot of delicate gadgets and a great deal of money – each *A-4* cost about £6,300 or $25,000. In late 1939, with his Panzer columns getting ready for a spring offensive, Hitler was not convinced that the *A-4* should ever go beyond the drawing board stage.

The spring of 1940 brought the Wehrmacht and armoured divisions out from behind the Siegfried Line. German forces rolled through Belgium and Holland and France. Paris was occupied in mid-June. The Wehrmacht waited at the edge of the Channel for the signal to invade Britain. With the war going so well, it looked as though the rockets would not be needed.

But the Luftwaffe lost the Battle of Britain, and the *A-4* project was back in business. Although Hitler still blew hot and cold about the missiles, they were given top priority. Test firing the *A-4* began in March 1942, but these shots did nothing to bolster Hitler's confidence in the rockets. The first *A-4* blew up. Three months later a second rocket rolled and twisted crazily after lift-off and crashed into the Baltic. Two months after this another *A-4* blew up just after launching.

Finally, on 3rd October 1942, the fourth *A-4* made a graceful ascent from its launch stand which was filmed by a battery of cameras. The black-and-white painted missile performed flawlessly throughout its flight and splashed down on target in the Baltic Sea, 118 miles downrange. Both Walter Dornberger and Wernher von Braun breathed a sigh of relief. There was still a lot of testing and experimenting to be done, but at least they now had one success they could build on.

While the tests went on, neither Dornberger, by now a colonel, nor Wernher von Braun heard anything from Adolf Hitler, which was all right with them – no news was good news. Then, one day in March 1943, Munitions Minister Albert Speer came to

Peenemünde and dropped a thunderbolt. Speer told Dornberger of a bad dream Hitler had about the missiles: that no *A-4* would ever reach England. The rocket programme was in danger; Hitler's dream would be excuse enough to cancel everything.

Munitions Minister Speer himself backed the project, which was one reason why Hitler did not call it off. But Dornberger and von Braun feared that *Der Führer* would one day, for some idiotic reason or maybe for no reason at all, cut off all funds for their research. They had not done all that work and spent months of effort just to have it all thrown out. So, they decided to do something to help their own cause.

On 7th July 1943 Dornberger, von Braun and another scientist climbed aboard a Heinkel He111 bomber and were flown over low cloud cover to Hitler's 'Wolf's Lair' in East Prussia. They brought along some scale models of *A-4* launchers and a few coloured graphs and drawings. As the *pièce de résistance*, they had a colour film of last October's first successful *A-4* launch.

Hitler had been holed up in East Prussia for quite some time, directing the stagnant Russian Front. He looked seriously ill. His hands trembled, and the grey-green uniform tunic he wore gave his waxy face the complexion of a corpse. Isolated from the rest of the world and under the influence of drugs, Hitler had begun to lose touch with reality. He could no longer clearly draw the line between what was real and what existed only in his own brain. In this state of mind, Hitler would have been susceptible to any grand strategy or fabulous new weapon. The more fantastic the idea, the heartier his approval.

Along with members of the High Command, Hitler inspected the models and drawings. After that, everybody sat down to see what else the rocket men had to show them.

Wernher von Braun personally narrated the film, describing every point and detail with infectious enthusiasm. The film began with the 46-foot-long missile being wheeled to its launch stand, then showed the pre-firing preparations and, as the climax, the launch.

White and yellow flame and smoke billowed from the *A-4*'s stern; slowly at first but with increasing speed, the missile began to rise. The cameras followed its ascent and stayed right with the rocket until it punched through the white layer of overcast, travelling faster than sound.

Dornberger and von Braun had designed the film for dramatic impact, and it certainly did its job. After the lights came back on, Hitler sat still for a moment; then he got up, shook hands with the three rocket men and actually thanked them for their work. A moment later, he came close to apologising for not having recognised the rocket's potential, declaring that there would have been no war in 1939 if he had long-range guided missiles.

Hitler's enthusiasm was now almost beyond control. He demanded von Braun and Dornberger build a rocket that would carry ten tons of explosives. When the scientists explained that it would take at least five years to develop such a missile, Hitler ordered that mammoth concrete launching bunkers for the *A-4*'s be built at once.

Walter Dornberger, who had been promoted to general in March 1943, favoured small, mobile launchers. A bunker the size of the one Hitler wanted would make an almost unmissable target for Allied bombers, he argued. But Hitler would not listen. Every bomb dropped on the launching sites would be one less on the Ruhr Valley cities. Hitler's orders prevailed.

The demonstration accomplished what von Braun and Dornberger wanted, though. The rocket project was once again given top priority. Late in 1943 the *A-4* went into mass production.

While the Army was developing its long-range rockets, the Air Force was becoming increasingly jealous of the tests and experiments at Peenemünde. Hermann Göring's Luftwaffe had once been the Third Reich's foremost striking power. Now, not only had the air arm been reduced to a defensive role, sending up fighters while the British and Americans launched bombing attacks, but it had to sit back and watch while the Army prepared to attack London.

The Luftwaffe's anxiety was eased in no small way by the pilotless Flying Bomb. The Flying Bomb, which would be known as the V-1, was far simpler and much less sophisticated than the *A-4* rocket, but simplicity was its strong point. It could be manufactured in less time and for far less money than the delicate and complex guided missile.

A V-1 Flying Bomb resembled a small airplane with a stove pipe over its tail and no cockpit. Its overall length was just over 25 feet, with a wing span of 17½ feet. Standard 80 octane gasoline fuelled its jet engine, which was housed in the 'stove pipe' assembly, the same fuel used by trucks and lorries. It was easy to build, cheap – £120; $500 – and carried a one-ton warhead, the same as the *A-4* rocket.

Launching was done by catapult. The catapult's piston gave the bomb its initial thrust, pushing it along the launching rails until airborne. After firing, the bomb flew along a pre-set, gyroscope-controlled course.

Accuracy was not the Flying Bomb's best-known feature, but it was accurate enough to hit a target as large as Greater London. It was designed as a cheap, simple machine to hit back at the enemy without risking the depleted reserves of the Luftwaffe's bomber fleet. This was all that Hitler wanted.

Compared with the months and months of trials involving the *A-4*, only nine months passed between the beginning of work on the Flying Bomb project in March 1942 and the first successful launching on Christmas Eve.

The early months of 1943 saw intensive testing continue with the Flying Bomb, which was officially known as *FZG 76* – *Flakzielgerät* (Anti-Aircraft Target Device) 76 – to throw enemy spies off the track. By the summer of the same year, plans were already being drawn up for the Flying Bomb assault against England.

One of the issues still to be decided was what kind of launching site the Flying Bomb should have. There was the same argument as with the *A-4* rockets – some favoured huge concrete emplacements, while others proposed smaller sites. As head of the Luftwaffe, it was up to Hermann Göring to decide. Reichsmarschall Göring compromised, ordering four elaborate concrete bunkers and 96 smaller sites begun immediately.

Next, men had to be trained for handling and firing the Flying Bomb. A new Luftwaffe unit was formed in August 1943 called *Flakregiment* 155(W); the anti-aircraft designation was, once again, aimed at deceiving enemy intelligence.

This new unit was placed under the command of Luftwaffe

'... a small aircraft with a stove pipe over its tail.' Resting on the end of its launching ramp, a Flying Bomb is prepared for firing by its crew

'... by a sea coast, and secluded.' A 1943 photograph of the rocket workshops at the Peenemünde missile complex.

Colonel Max Wachtel, who had been in charge of all experimental Flying Bomb shots. Colonel Wachtel was instructed to get his men ready for firing the bomb under actual combat conditions. Wachtel took his orders to heart; his *Flakregiment* began its exercises within days of the unit's creation. From the western side of Peenemünde, the launching crews began readying the small, jet-propelled planes and firing them downrange over the Baltic Sea in quick succession.

All that was missing now were the Flying Bombs themselves. Colonel Wachtel's men had been firing early experimental models; by September, all of these had been fired in practice shots. A new lot arrived early in September, a modified version of the early model, but not enough to make much difference. By October only 38 of these missiles had been delivered.

Grand things had been expected from the manufacturers of the Flying Bomb: estimates of 5,000 per month had been bandied about at one point. But the Volkswagen plant at Fallersleben, near Hamburg, where the bombs were being manufactured, was falling far short. Only 38 Flying Bombs were being turned out each month.

The endless series of bugs that plagued the Flying Bomb was at the root of the production slowdown. Crashing just after launching was the most persistent problem. Sometimes the bomb would travel only a few yards from its test catapult before smashing into the ground. No sooner did the technicians at Volkswagen iron out one flaw than another would spring up. The mass-production timetable was rolled back again and again. Finally, the end of March 1944 was announced as the date when the FZG 76 would go into full production.

Volkswagen's engineers had called their shot. By March 1944, an operational model of the Flying Bomb was ready. In April, 1,000 of them rolled off the assembly line; in May, 1,500 more came out; and in June, 2,500.

Adolf Hitler was kept informed of the Flying Bomb's progress. When he was satisfied that enough of the missiles had been stockpiled, in mid-May, Hitler ordered a massive assault against Britain to begin within the month.

This order came as a very rude shock to Colonel Max Wachtel. Colonel Wachtel had been waiting for some kind of word at Saleux,

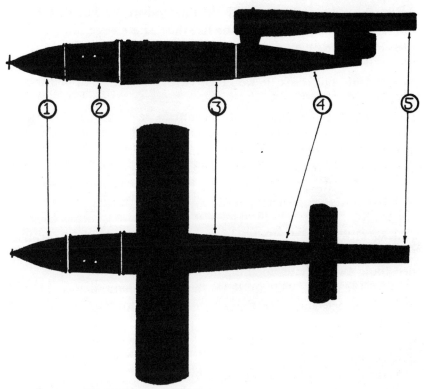

FZG-76 (V-1) Flying Bomb
1. Nose Section contains compass mechanism and 'windmill' device, plus pressure fuse for detonating warhead.
2. Warhead consists of 2,031 lbs of Trialen aluminium explosive. Fusing system made up of two external fuses – one impact and one 'delay' fuse – plus two internal pressure fuses and one electric fuse.
3. Two compressed air bottles for operating gyroscope, plus fuel tank. The object protruding beneath the fuselage is the launching lug, which engages with the catapult's firing piston.
4. Gyroscope and auto-pilot mechanisms, which operated the rudder and elevators.
5. Housing containing pulse-jet engine.

across the Channel from southern England in the Pas de Calais, but he wasn't expecting anything like this. There were still weeks of preparations to be made before the launchings could begin. Most of his *Flakregiment*'s equipment hadn't even been delivered yet. Wachtel did not think he would be ready until the end of June at the earliest.

But the High Command didn't want to hear it; there had been too many excuses already. Colonel Wachtel had been given a specific date to begin the attack, and he was expected to do as he was told. The date set down in Colonel Wachtel's orders for opening the attack on London was 10th June. That gave Wachtel less than a week; the orders were delivered on 4th June 1944.

During all this time, while Usedom Island and northern France churned with activity, Allied Intelligence was, slowly but surely, becoming aware that something unusual was going on.

On 15th May 1942 an RAF flight lieutenant flew a photo-reconnaissance run over the north German port of Kiel. After completing his assignment the pilot still had a few shots left in his camera, so he decided to make a pass over the airfield at Peenemünde. Usedom Island wasn't far from Kiel, and maybe something interesting was going on over there.

The reconnaissance photos didn't show anything unusual at the airfield, but they did reveal some 'elliptical earthworks' – the firing stands for the *A-4* rockets. Since none of the photo interpreters had been told to look out for any odd-shaped emplacements, however, the photos were numbered and buried away in the files. The oval objects on them were ignored.

With programmes as large as the Vengeance Weapon projects, which involved many thousands of people – labourers, technicians, clerks – it was impossible to keep things a secret forever. Word was bound to leak out sooner or later.

Early in 1943 Polish manual labourers at Peenemünde began noticing a heavy, vibrating noise that came from the north-west part of Usedom Island. It was a curious, pulsing sound, larger and more powerful than any aircraft engine they had ever heard. At other times, while moving earth to make room for another launching site, they would catch a glimpse of a small aeroplane, with short wings and a flaming tail, flying out to sea.

The labourers talked about what they had seen and heard among themselves. As the strange sights and sounds continued, the talking increased. Eventually, the labourers' stories got around to another Pole, who brought food and supplies over to Peenemünde from the German mainland. When he got back to the mainland, this Pole mentioned the tales he had been told about the strange aircraft to friends and acquaintances. The story spread. The word began to drift around, in bars and in shops and on the street. By and by, the word reached the ear of a member of the Polish Underground.

In London, the Bureau of the Polish General Staff received a message in the spring of 1943: something mysterious was happening at Usedom Island in the Baltic. This contact was passed on to British Intelligence. British Intelligence asked for more details.

Other messages were received from scattered sources – underground units in Occupied Europe, intelligence agents inside Germany – which kept mentioning secret weapons and Peenemünde. Finally, it dawned on the War Office Intelligence Branch that something must be up. And so they appointed one man, Duncan Sandys, to investigate the possibility of the long-range rocket development, which these reports kept hinting at – no mention was made of the Flying Bomb. Sandys was to report directly to Winston Churchill and the War Cabinet with his findings.

Duncan Sandys, only 35 years old, had been appointed to this post over the head of several senior ministers. There were more than just a few protests over his appointment. Some argued that Sandys was not a scientist, and had no business to hold such a post. Others angrily hinted at favouritism; Sandys was married to Winston Churchill's daughter Diana.

But Duncan Sandys was uniquely qualified. In 1940 he had been in command of a unit which fired the small, solid-fuelled 'Z' anti-aircraft rocket – the only rocket unit in the Army – and remained until a car crash ended his military service. After recovering from the accident, Sandys joined the Ministry of Supply, and became responsible for all weapons research and development. Duncan Sandys was one of the few people in Britain who had background with weapons research as well as practical experience with rockets.

The investigation of the suspected Peenemünde rocket project began a few days after Sandys' appointment. Almost immediately, unknown to Sandys, it bogged down. Most of the 'evidence' presented to him was either misleading or else totally false.

Some of the material considered includes: a report on the *A-4* by a German technical expert who made up his information as he went along, claiming, among other things, that the rocket weighed 100 tons; some muddled and not very helpful intelligence reports; a reconnaissance photo of Peenemünde that was misinterpreted; a Flying Bomb launching ramp was labelled a 'dredge pipe'.

Finally, late in June, Sandys got what he was looking for. A photo-reconnaissance Mosquito snapped a series of sharp, clear pictures of Peenemünde. Photo analysts discovered two rockets, which had been caught lying on their sides out in the open. Also, there were several 'odd-looking' aircraft which appeared to be jet-propelled.

Duncan Sandys wasn't all that interested in the strange jet planes, but he was relieved that he could at last provide proof, visual, concrete proof, of rockets at Peenemünde. Sandys advised that a bombing raid be carried out against Peenemünde as soon as possible; destroying the sites was the most direct way of combating the missiles.

It took over a month of debate and argument before the War Cabinet was convinced that an air raid was really necessary. After that, another couple of weeks passed before the moon was right; a bright, full moon would be needed for the bomb-aimers to find their targets.

On the night of 17th August 1943, while a few Mosquito path-finders dropped flares on Berlin to decoy the Luftwaffe's night fighters, 597 Lancaster and Halifax bombers toggled their loads over the rocket centre. The sortie cost the RAF forty aircraft and 240 men, but the bombing had been accurate. Large fires were observed within the target area.

Strike photos taken by photo-reconnaissance on the morning after the raid showed a concentration of bomb damage. Several fires were still burning fiercely. The bomber crews were congratulated for their accuracy, and damage reports gave detailed accounts of widespread destruction. The War Cabinet was satisfied that Peenemünde had been destroyed.

Walter Dornberger, now a major-general, had another opinion. Dornberger estimated that the rocket programme had been set back only about six weeks. Although the bombing raid had churned up an impressive amount of rubble, most of the bombs had fallen on the technicians' housing development. Only one important, irreplaceable rocket scientist had been killed. Seven, hundred and fifty others also had died, but 600 of these were Polish labourers and Russian prisoners of war.

General Dornberger decided to use the raid to his own advantage. Everything would be left as it was, all bomb damage in place; to a snooping photo-reconnaissance plane, it would look as though Peenemünde were lifeless and barren, unable to carry on with operations.

The ruse worked. Allied bombers did not return for nine months, while the rocket programme went into high gear.

In the autumn of 1943, those odd-looking jet planes popped up again. This time, there were some odd-looking buildings to go with them.

Reconnaissance pilots had picked up several sites in northern France, mostly in Normandy and the Pas de Calais. Each of these sites was identical, made up of the same number of unusual looking buildings. One of these buildings was long and narrow, curving slightly at one end; photo analysts decided that they looked like the side view of a ski, and called these places 'ski sites'. Besides looking alike, the ski sites had something else in common – they all had gently sloping ramps that lined up exactly on London.

Intelligence experts thought that these long, sloping ramps had something to do with the long-range rockets. But someone remembered seeing that kind of ramp before – in the reconnaissance photos of Peenemünde airfield from May 1942. The photos were dug up and, sure enough, there was that same long, inclined ramp.

One of the WAAF photo interpreters looked through a magnifying glass at the ramp and saw a small, propellerless aeroplane on it. After a closer look, she could see that the plane had no cockpit. The secret of the ski sites was out.

Less than a week later, during the first week of December 1943, the first air strikes were carried out against the launch sites by the RAF and US Army Air Force. These attacks were known by the general code-word *Crossbow*, but to the bomber crews of the US 8th and 9th Air Forces they were called 'Noball' missions.

These Noball sorties were treated the same as any other air raid, except that nobody was told what the target was during pre-flight briefings. 'We didn't actually know what we were bombing,' recounted the pilot of a B-26 Marauder. This was a radical departure from the usual routine. Normally, the Primary Target was the first thing mentioned, described in great detail by the Intelligence Officer. The secrecy didn't help anyone's nerves.

Another thing that shook everybody up was the fact that these Noball targets were heavily defended by anti-aircraft fire, which was 'usually pretty accurate', to put it politely. Before one sortie, the men of a B-17 Flying Fortress unit were given elaborately detailed instructions on how to make their bomb run; as usual, the target itself was not named. 'Don't screw up on this one,' the Intelligence Officer concluded the briefing, 'or you'll get your asses shot off.'

Crossbow and Noball missions continued into the spring of 1944, even though, unknown to Allied Intelligence, the ski sites and one of the large concrete bunkers had been abandoned. The mammoth concrete bunker at Watten, in northern France, which Hitler had insisted upon, had been bombed out of existence by 185 B-17 Flying Fortresses. The ski sites were kept in repair, but this was only to make them seem operational to prying reconnaissance planes. While Bomber Command and the US Army Air Force were busy attacking the empty ski sites, Colonel Max Wachtel and his *Flakregiment* 155(W) were making other preparations in the Normandy and Pas de Calais.

In spite of all their efforts, the British and American air forces had not been able to stop the Vengeance Weapon projects. After Peenemünde was bombed, many of the test centre's most vital buildings were scattered throughout Germany. The *A-4* rocket factory was moved into a huge, complex network of tunnels underneath the Hartz Mountains in Central Germany.

Inside the mile-long tunnels under the mountains, where bombs could not penetrate, tests were continuing on the *A-4*. Rocket technicians were facing a seemingly endless flow of problems, just as the Flying Bomb technicians had done. Only the Flying Bomb was a relatively simple machine, so its flaws were relatively simple to correct. With the incredibly complex *A-4*, however, making the necessary changes and adjustments in the combustion system, guidance system, and a myriad of other mechanisms took months of time and effort. Modifications were made almost continually on the thousands of bugs that infested the *A-4*, but test rockets kept on exploding in mid-air or breaking up before impact. Adding to the burden were the pressures from Armed Forces High Command, who were always asking how soon the rockets would be ready for use against England.

While the *A-4* missile was causing a wide variety of headaches at Peenemünde and in the Harz Mountains, the Flying Bombs continued to roll out of the Volkswagen plant at Fallersleben. The High Command was becoming impatient about these also, asking when the first shots at London would be launched.

Colonel Max Wachtel and *Flakregiment* 155(W) were still waiting in the Pas de Calais. Wachtel's launch units still had no Flying Bombs, no launching rails, and no equipment. In spite of this, Headquarters was eager for him to begin launching the robot bombs against London as soon as possible. On 4th June Wachtel told his commanding officers that he would not be able to begin operations before 20th June, which made them unhappy and angry.

Headquarters did not think that they were being unreasonable in ordering Colonel Wachtel to begin launching on 10th June, the date set down in his orders. According to Headquarters, the launch sites were already half prepared. Colonel Wachtel and his *Flakregiment* would be using new launching ramps called 'modified sites' – light, pre-fabricated catapults; small and quickly assembled. The ski sites and concrete bunkers had proven too vulnerable to Allied bombers; these new ramps were built with camouflage and concealment in mind. Concrete foundations for the ramps had been poured long before. Everything else would be assembled when needed. But so far, nothing had been delivered.

On 6th June the situation changed abruptly. Reports on the invasion of the Normandy beaches kept coming through all day long. That night the first shipment of steel launching catapults arrived.

For the next five days, Colonel Wachtel and his crews worked day in and day out to assemble the catapults. They had to do everything themselves, from conducting tests on the new sites to unloading trains.

Some things were beyond Wachtel's control. Allied air strikes had intensified since D-Day, hampering the arrival of supplies. Trains were strafed and de-railed. Frequently sections of the new steel launching ramps had to be delivered by road, travelling at night through the black-out to avoid enemy fighter-bombers. Sometimes, the ramps ended up at the wrong place.

Colonel Wachtel's superior officers had relented a little, and rolled back the launch date by two days. The Flying Bomb attack was now scheduled to begin at 11.40 on the night of the 12th. Because of the delays caused by enemy air attacks, however, even this two day respite was not enough. On the night of the 12th, Colonel Wachtel informed his immediate superior, General Erich Heinemann, that the launch sites were still not ready.

Wachtel and his men had assembled fifty-five of the steel catapults on their cement foundations. But no safety equipment had arrived yet; neither had fuel for the Flying Bombs and other essential supplies. None of the catapults had been tested, either.

Over the telephone Colonel Wachtel asked for permission to postpone the launch. He was given an hour's reprieve. But that hour passed, and still things were not ready; firing time was rolled back again. Finally, 3.00 of the morning of the 13th was agreed as zero hour. If Wachtel was not ready by that time, the attack would be postponed. Also, the Colonel knew, he could be brought before a court of inquiry for failure to carry out his orders; loss of rank and pay were among the punishments that could be dealt him by such a court.

The mass attack called for by Headquarters was almost certainly out of the question, but Colonel Wachtel knew that he would have to launch some sort of effort before daybreak.

CHAPTER TWO

'Hit by a Powder Puff'

Things couldn't have been worse. To Unteroffizier Otto Neuchel, it was a classic case of One Damn Thing After Another. Everything was going wrong. First, there hadn't been enough fuel for all the Flying Bombs. Next, it was discovered that there would not be enough equipment to go around. When the piston release mechanism on Neuchel's untested catapult broke down, it could not be repaired – there were no spare parts.

As the appointed launching time, 3.00 on the morning of June 13th, approached, Colonel Max Wachtel's *Flakregiment* was still hard at work. Unteroffizier Neuchel and everyone else were doing their best to prepare as many Flying Bombs as possible for firing. But under the circumstances there wasn't very much the men could accomplish.

By 3.30 a.m. only ten of the fifty-five firing ramps were ready; Unteroffizier Neuchel's was not among the ten. Neuchel felt highly frustrated over not being able to take part in the launch. After wrestling with that balking ramp all night, actually firing a few Flying Bombs would have been a welcome relief for the stocky twenty year-old.

Months of practice made the pre-launch procedure a set routine. First, the pilotless plane's fuel tanks were checked, to make sure they had been topped off. Following this, its wings were attached – the wings were folded over the fuselage to make storing and moving the bombs easier, and were quickly mounted at the last minute. After assembly, the bombs were aligned precisely with their firing ramps – which were pointed directly at London – and gyrocompass mechanisms set at zero.

The Flying Bomb, now ready for launching, was moved onto its firing site. After being loaded onto its catapult, a lug on the underside of the fuselage was engaged to the catapult's firing piston. When the piston was released it shot forward, slinging the bomb off the launching rails in the same way that a jet is catapulted off an aircraft carrier's flight deck.

With the stubby-winged Flying Bomb poised for take-off, the launching crew took cover inside the control 'bunker', a heavily armoured trailer that housed the catapult's firing controls. Unteroffizier Neuchel's catapult was still broken down, and he elected to watch the launch from a safe distance. When everyone was out of the way, the firing officer gave an order. A small lever on the control panel's instrument panel was pulled, and the Flying Bomb's pulse-jet engine came to life with a throbbing, ear-numbing roar.

This simple jet engine was the Flying Bomb's unique feature. Housed outside the fuselage, above the tail, the jet is usually described as looking like either a stove pipe or a giant blow torch.

At the front of the engine housing was a system of intake flaps. These flaps opened at the beginning of the engine's cycle, drawing air into the combustion chamber and mixing the air with 80 octane fuel. In the second stage, the flaps closed and the fuel-and-oxygen mixture was ignited. A burst of hot exhaust shot out from the rear of the engine with a tremendous flash, pushing the machine forward. Immediately after ignition the flaps opened again, forcing air into the combustion chamber and repeating the cycle.

All this sounds very long and drawn-out, but this simple jet could complete up to 500 cycles every minute, giving the Flying Bomb speeds well over 300 miles per hour. The engine's open-close, open-close system also gave the Flying Bomb its distinctive *duv-duv-duv*-sound that Londoners would soon come to recognise.

After listening for a moment to make sure that the engine was not malfunctioning, the firing officer gave the order to launch. A second lever was pulled, releasing the catapult's piston.

The Flying Bomb lurched forward, shot along the length of steel rail, and jumped uncertainly into the night sky. It was not a very graceful sight – like watching an ungainly bird being propelled into flight by a sudden gust of wind. Unteroffizier Otto Neuchel thought the bombs clumsy and awkward, but was fascinated by the sight just the same.

Nine more of the bombs bolted from their catapults during the

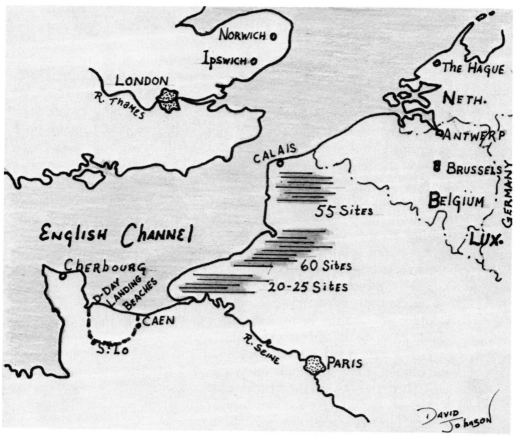

Between 135 and 140 Flying Bomb launching ramps were in position along the
Pas de Calais by mid-June — pointed at London. West of the launch sites are the
D-Day beaches.

next half-hour, between about 3.30 and 4.00. Unteroffizier Neuchel watched each one of the small aircraft leave its ramp, brilliant flashes of fire trailing from their exhaust.

Four of the shots failed – the Flying Bombs fell to earth just after firing, sending Neuchel diving for cover. One of the crashed bombs even failed to explode. The other three burst on impact with an awesome concussion – Neuchel doesn't remember a 'bang' at all, just a terrible force that rushed right over him and hurt his eardrums.

Six of the ten shots went as planned. All eyes looked on as the pilotless machines took off; their glowing engines and pulsating roar, trailing off into the darkness, exhilarated and sobered each spectator.

After all the drills and training and preparation, this was the time everyone had been waiting for. Unteroffizier Neuchel had seen dozens of practice shots at Peenemünde, but these launchings made him feel different somehow. He knew why. Tonight the bombs would not come down on some aiming point in the Baltic Sea, but would crash into the enemy's densely populated capital, carrying nearly 2,000 lbs of high explosives.

Two of the six successfully launched Flying Bombs crashed into the Channel. The remaining four continued on their north-north-westerly course toward the Kentish cliffs and, ultimately, London.

A clever but not very accurate mechanism would send the Flying Bombs into their final dive over the target. On the nose of each bomb was a 'windmill' device, looking like a small replica of a two-bladed aircraft propeller. As the Flying Bomb rushed through the air, the miniature airscrew turned, pinwheel-like, by the machine's forward motion.

This 'windmill' connected up with the bomb's auto-pilot; after a pre-set number of revolutions the windmill tripped the diving controls, veering the bomb earthwards at a steep angle. The mechanism was set by the launching crew, based on careful calculations involving the Flying Bomb's speed and the distance to the target, before launching.

Any number of factors could undo this already none-too-precise system. Headwinds or tailwinds would alter the machine's airspeed, ruining the most carefully worked-out calculations. The mechanism itself was not flawless. It might go haywire and send the bomb plunging into the Channel, miles short of land, as had happened twice already. Or it might not work at all, causing the Flying Bomb to overfly the whole of London and keep going until all fuel was gone.

The aiming point was Tower Bridge, which linked the blitzed London Docks on the River Thames's north bank with the Borough of Southwark on the south bank. It would take only about twenty-five minutes for the bombs to reach their target – if everything worked and went according to plan.

American intelligence worker Richard Baker was awakened by the air raid siren at about 4 a.m. He and three of his colleagues were supposed to be standing fire watch on their office building, located in Brook Street in London's West End. But there hadn't been anything happening, so the firewatchers curled up in the bathroom and went to sleep.

When they heard the sirens, Baker and his three mates pulled their clothes on and went up on the roof. Nobody saw anything, but after a few minutes, Baker heard what sounded like a single anti-aircraft gun going off. After a while the All Clear sounded. Everybody went back down to the bathroom to get some more sleep.

Five minutes later, the sirens went again. Richard Baker and the other three firewatchers once again got up, dressed hastily, and went back up on the roof. They stayed there for the rest of the pre-dawn hours – until the All Clear sounded – bewildered by the lack of air activity.

A few miles north of Brook Street, in Cholmley Gardens, West Hampstead, Mrs Gwladys Cox was also awakened by the sirens. 'I have just returned to bed after a brief alert ...' she wrote at 4.15 a.m. 'I had just time to get up and dress when the All Clear went.'

At 4.35 Mrs Cox made another entry in her diary: 'I had to get up again and dress for another alert.'

The same thing happened all over London: an alert, followed by the All Clear, then another alert that lasted over an hour. When the sirens first sounded, most people simply sat up in bed and listened

– the first evidence of an air raid was the steady *drumm-drumm-drumm* of the approaching Luftwaffe bombers, then came the loud, penetrating bark of the local anti-aircraft batteries. Hearing nothing, people opened the blackout curtains for a look out of the window. There was nothing to be seen, especially at four-thirty in the morning, except a thousand stars that glowed and sparkled above the blacked-out streets.

It was all very puzzling. The first alert could have been caused by a lone enemy reconnaissance plane, or even by a mechanical failure. But that long second alert was no mistake. Being awakened out of a sound sleep was bad enough, but not knowing what was going on was even worse.

There were a few who had observed something. As the four Flying Bombs passed over south-eastern England, some people heard an unusual chug-chugging noise, sounding like an old jalopy sputtering up a hill. They looked up and saw a fiery streak rush by at low altitude. Most didn't know what to make of it. Some thought it must be some strange new kind of aeroplane. A young schoolboy in East London thought it was a Luftwaffe raider on fire.

Only one Flying Bomb hit London. It landed and exploded in Bethnal Green, East London, about three miles from its Tower Bridge aiming point. The explosion killed three people and knocked out a railway bridge.

The other three came down far wide of their target. The closest was at Gravesend, Kent, about 22 miles east of Tower Bridge, while the remaining two hit Sevenoaks, Kent and Cuckfield, Sussex, many miles short. No one was killed or injured except by the Bethnal Green bomb.

At Air Defence of Great Britain Headquarters in Stanmore, Middlesex, no one was at all surprised or puzzled by the early morning goings-on. Stanmore knew that the Flying Bombs were coming almost as soon as they were launched, and had been tracking the machines since the bombs were on the French side of the Channel.

During the Battle of Britain and the Blitz in 1940 and 1941, Stanmore had been called simply Headquarters, Fighter Command. It was from here, just north-west of London, that the battle against the Luftwaffe had been directed.

Radar stations along the Channel coast gave the first warning of enemy air activity, picking up the formations while they were still forming-up over the Continent. These contacts were passed along to Stanmore where, in the Filter Room, the enemy's heading and speed would be traced across a huge table map of Great Britain – the map itself was as large as a good-sized room. Women's Auxiliary Air Force plotters pushed red metal arrows, each arrow representing a flight of intruders, northward towards London on the great map. From an overhead gallery, the Operations staff watched the proceedings. When the red arrows were committed, the Operations Commander telephoned a battery of police stations, air raid posts, and airfields, giving the alert and scrambling fighters to the attack.

Tonight, the ritual repeated itself. Chain Home (Low) Radar Stations at Beachy Head, Fairlight, and Dover, along the Channel coast of Kent, picked up the first of the Flying Bombs at about 4 a.m. The Chain Home (Low) stations were designed especially for the detection of low-flying aircraft. Although these stations had a range of only about 50 miles, they were tailor-made for picking up the Flying Bombs, which approached at altitudes of 2,500 feet and below.

After Stanmore received the first enemy contact, the WAAF plotters, manipulating their long, magnet-tipped plotting rods, pushed a single red arrow north-westward across the Filter Room's map. As the first Flying Bomb neared the Kentish coast, the 'red' alert was sounded – tearing along at 330 miles per hour, the bomb would take only about fifteen minutes to reach London.

When it flew inland, 'behind' the radar installations, the Flying Bomb's flaring exhaust was picked up visually by Royal Observer Corps outposts. At about 4.15, Stanmore received an excited one-word message, 'Diver!' – the code word signalling the appearance of the secret weapon – from an observer post in Kent. The bomb hit and blew up in Gravesend, Kent, at 4.18, causing no casualties.

Because Colonel Max Wachtel and his men were having so much trouble launching the Flying Bombs, the radar screens along the south coast were clear for a few minutes while Flakregiment 155(W) prepared for the next firing. When Beachy Head and Fairlight stations picked up more incoming machines about ten minutes later, the 'red' alert was sounded again.

There was little else for Stanmore to do except track the Flying Bombs and issue air raid alerts. Night fighters were scrambled to shoot down the intruders, but the Flying Bombs were through the defences before any fighters could reach their stations.

Intelligence had warned that Flying Bomb attacks might be expected at any time, but Air Defence Headquarters had been led to believe that nothing would take place before the end of June. This attack caught everyone by surprise.

Air Marshal Roderick M. Hill, the Commander of Air Defence, was not terribly surprised by the appearance of the Flying Bombs, but he was disappointed and disheartened. For months, the RAF and US Army Air Force had carried out hundreds of bombing and strafing missions against Flying Bomb emplacements. But in spite of all that, the machines had not been stopped.

As far as London was concerned, the early morning attack never even happened. None of the Wednesday newspapers made any mention of the Flying Bombs, and since very few people actually saw the bomb that hit Bethnal Green, nobody had any idea of what had gone on. There was a lot of grumbling about being roused out of bed by the two alerts, but no one realised that they had been attacked by a new German secret weapon.

Winston Churchill's War Cabinet had been thoroughly briefed on the enemy air activity, however, and had a great deal to talk about. Not everyone agreed on what had actually taken place, though, or what to do about it.

Some of the Cabinet members thought the launch was nothing but a bluff, a diversion to draw attention away from the fighting in Normandy. An opening salvo of 400 Flying Bombs had been predicted at one point; when only four arrived, there was much light talk about what a false alarm the feared Vengeance Weapon turned out to be. One American intelligence officer doesn't recall feeling particularly elated by the weak showing, only let down. 'It was like bracing for a solid punch in the jaw,' he would later write, 'and getting hit by a powder puff.'

Duncan Sandys knew better. He and other experts warned the

Cabinet not to dismiss the matter so lightly. There had been increased activity in the Pas de Calais area during the past week; all that work wasn't being done to prepare four diversionary shots. The Germans across the Channel were capable of a much larger effort than this.

Sandys' plea fell on deaf ears. The War Cabinet was no longer all that worried about the Flying Bombs, and passed their new evaluation on to the Allied Expeditionary Force's chief, Air Marshal Trafford Leigh-Mallory.

The War Cabinet's opinion had immediate results. An air strike of 3,000 B-17 Flying Fortress sorties had been planned against the Flying Bomb sites. But in light of the feeble Flying Bomb attack, these 3,000 sorties were reduced to 1,000.

Unteroffizier Otto Neuchel had never worked so hard in his life. His commander, Colonel Max Wachtel, was under pressure to begin the full-scale attack on London as soon as possible; as always, the commanding officer's problems were passed down to the junior officers and enlisted men. For the past two days, Neuchel and everybody else in the bomb launch crews had sweated and strained to get all Flying Bomb catapults operational.

Things were even more hectic and back-breaking than they had been the week before. The equipment that had been lacking on Monday night was delivered all at once, fuel, spare parts and tools. There was even a shipment of tinned fruit, a welcome arrival. After it was all unloaded, the men went to work on the launching ramps. All fifty-five ramps were checked, repaired, and finally test-fired to make sure everything worked. Since Monday, 12th June, nobody had more than a few hours' sleep and an occasional bite to eat. If anyone sat down for even a moment, there was always some officer coming around to raise hell.

By Thursday the 15th, every catapult had been fired and passed inspection. Colonel Wachtel informed his superiors that the launching ramps were ready. Colonel Wachtel could now breathe a sigh of relief, but Unteroffizier Neuchel was just as glad that all the toil and bother was finished. For the first time in three days, he would be able to sit down and have a smoke without being bullied and harassed.

The rest period was a short one. At about 7 p.m., Colonel Wachtel received a phone call from the headquarters of his commanding officer, Lieutenant General Erich Heinemann. Over the telephone, Wachtel received his orders, which he immediately passed along to all firing units. *Flakregiment* 155 (W) was to open fire on 'Target Forty-Two' – the code-word for London – at 11.15.

Eleven-fifteen was still a long way off, but there were a lot of things to be done before firing time. The Flying Bombs had to be rolled out and fitted with their wings. Then the catapults would have their camouflage removed, and the bombs' gyro mechanisms set on line with the target. Nothing was being left to chance. After Monday night's fiasco, it all had better go right this time.

By the time zero hour approached, all of the catapults were primed and ready for the big moment. On the rear of each rested a small, complacent-looking pilotless aeroplane, its nose pointing toward the northern horizon. Lieutenant General Heinemann had dropped in on Colonel Wachtel's command post in Saleux to keep track of things, but there was nothing to be alarmed about. The launch was expected to go well tonight. Even the weather was co-operating. Low cloud was already beginning to form overhead, perfect for the pilotless machines since the heavy weather would hinder Allied fighters.

The grey overcast lent a hazy white half-light to the landscape, blending the distant horizon with the clouds, making it impossible to tell where earth left off and sky began. Squatting on their firing ramps, the Flying Bombs seemed darker and somewhat larger in the milky glow, magnified by both the diffused light and the mind's eye.

Unteroffizier Otto Neuchel went off by himself for a few moments, alone with his thoughts as he watched the deceptively peaceful scene. Everything and everyone around him was subdued, like the grey light. Even orders were given in a quiet, crisp tone of voice. But Neuchel could sense the tension underneath the calm. It reminded him of when he was back at school in Karlsruhe, in Germany's Black Forest, on the night before an important examination. As the final word to begin launching was awaited, he felt the pins-and-needles of excitement mingled with a strange, undefined feeling of foreboding.

The word came shortly after 11.00. At 11.16 the first of the Flying Bombs was launched, followed by the firing of all catapults. Neuchel could see the small jet propelled planes shooting into the overcast.

From inside the control trailer, Neuchel watched the Flying Bomb on his own ramp rising into life, its pulse jet harshly lighting up the landscape. After a few moments, which seemed like forever to the young *Unteroffizier*, the firing officer gave the order to launch.

The bomb slid effortlessly along its launch rails and thundered toward the grey clouds. Neuchel had the sinking feeling that the machine wasn't going to make it, that it would falter and crash – a feeling that would recur during almost every shot. The observation slits in the trailer allowed only a limited view, but Neuchel was able to see his Flying Bomb rumble heavily off to the north, sprouting a long, fiery tail.

Following the launch, the officers and men in Neuchel's unit took a moment to congratulate each other. It wasn't much of a ceremony, though; everybody was soon back at work. Another bomb was rolled up and readied for firing – wings attached, gyro mechanism set at zero. As he man-handled the Flying Bomb into position, Unteroffizier Neuchel wondered what happened to the bad feeling he had earlier. He felt no pangs of foreboding any longer, only satisfaction at having done a long, tedious job well.

CHAPTER THREE

'Like a Will-o'-the-Wisp in the Night'

'Hey! They got one! They got one!' At BBC Broadcasting House in London's West End, an American army officer suddenly began shouting excitedly and pointing out the window. Technical Sergeant Dick Dudley and everyone else in the room got up to see what all the noise was about. Sergeant Dudley arrived at the window just in time to see an aircraft rushing by, its tail brightly aflame. It looked as though the local anti-aircraft gunners had picked off a German bomber and set it on fire.

The air raid alert had already gone – 'deep throated, three-toned jobs that sounded as though they really meant it,' was one American's description of the sirens. When the Flying Bombs reached Greater London's southern boundary, the guns of the London Defence Region opened up. Anyone who missed the sirens was jolted awake by the roaring bark of the guns, which rattled windows and terrified small children. People who opened their blackout curtains were treated to the busy spectacle of searchlights trying to pick up the intruders – odd little aeroplanes with flaming tails – through a drizzly rain.

For all their sound and fury, the anti-aircraft guns were not doing much damage to the Flying Bombs. They never did very much damage anyway, not even at the height of the Blitz, when they used several thousand flak shells to bring down each enemy raider. Tonight, at least the gunners had an excuse. Their targets, zooming in at over 300 miles per hour, were on top of them and gone before fuses could be set properly.

Most of the shells burst far above the pilotless planes, exploding in brilliant white flashes. Bits of shell fragments cascaded down on streets and rooftops, breaking skylights and roofing tiles.

A few American servicemen stayed up to 'see the show', but most Londoners did not realise that anything extraordinary was going on. When the Alert went, everyone just assumed that it was only one more air raid.

In Cholmley Gardens, West Hampstead, Mrs Gwladys Cox and her husband Ralph were turned out of bed rather abruptly. 'We are in the middle of an air raid,' Mrs Cox noted, 'which started with a sudden loud gunfire behind our own flat just before midnight.' Some neighbours dropped in with the Coxes to pass the time. They all sat chatting quietly, waiting for the Alert to end.

Half an hour later, everybody was still sitting. 'We still await the All Clear and have had tea to keep ourselves awake – how *weary* we all are!'

Flying Bombs and pulse jets were unknown to Mr and Mrs Cox, who blamed the steady *duv-duv-duv* in the air on natural causes. 'The drumming of the atmosphere vibrations is incessant,' she said, 'and sometimes seems worse with a west wind, as tonight.'

Throughout the night the long alert continued – 2.00, 2.30, 3.00. At 3.45, Mrs Cox got her first look at the damage caused by the attack: 'Glow and fires to the east.' But she still assumed this was an all-night raid by the Luftwaffe, and wondered, 'Is the enemy after the docks and our embarkation of forces?'

It was impossible to sleep, except for brief cat-naps. One of Mrs Cox's remarks simply says, 'Heavy gun fire.' Only after the raid had gone on right through the night and into the pre-dawn hours did Mrs Cox suspect that this was not a conventional bombing attack.

'The alert is still on!' she exclaimed at 8.30 a.m. 'There must be something unusual afoot with such a long alert.'

Many more Londoners, especially people who lived south of the River Thames, had more than just suspicions to go on. The Flying Bombs, looking black against the light grey clouds, were plainly visible as they scuttled along.

An army doctor in the West End tried to keep tally of the bombs that passed over, but lost count when a hail of anti-aircraft shell fragments forced him to take cover. In Bexleyheath, Kent a young woman, hearing a 'chugging' noise, leaned out of her air raid shelter and saw 'what appeared to be a wooden cross in the sky with a flame at the back.'

'Go up! Go up!' Unteroffizier Otto Neuchel kept chanting under his breath each time his ramp let loose another Flying Bomb. 'We always held our breath whenever we sent one of those damn things up,' he would later recall.

There hadn't been any misfires yet, but he always had the fear that each bomb was going to go wrong and crash on take-off. This had happened several times already at other firing ramps – bombs had smashed into the ground just after launching, blowing up and wrecking the launch site.

Neuchel had been told to leave the control bunker earlier in the night; the trailer, he was told, was only for the firing officer and technicians. From the slit trench where he had taken cover, Neuchel could see and hear the explosions of the crashed Flying Bombs: violent flashes of light, followed by a powerful, roaring 'BOOOOM!' The 'terrible thunder and lightning' did not help to raise his spirits.

A lot of crashes certainly had occurred – forty-five, to be exact – but many more Flying Bombs left their ramps and headed toward London. By noon of 16th June, 244 missiles had been fired. Minus crashes, that left 199 airborne.

Unteroffizier Neuchel might have been apprehensive, but his commanding officer, Colonel Max Wachtel, could not have been happier. The launchings had gone off as planned, and Colonel Wachtel was nearly overcome with joy and relief. All the months of work and frustration had ended in success. To make sure that his superior officers knew about his achievement, Wachtel sent all of them jubilant, confident telegrams.

Colonel Wachtel's commander, Lieutenant General Erich Heinemann, heard nothing but good news. The launching ramps were continuing to fire steadily, right through the drizzly dawn hours. A report from a photo-reconnaissance plane mentioned bright fires burning within London. All was going well and, from the way things looked, would continue to go well.

Unteroffizier Neuchel also got some good news. Sometime during the early dawn, he and his crew were relieved; everyone was told that they could finally go off duty. To Neuchel, nothing ever sounded better. All he wanted now was several hours of uninterrupted sleep.

By morning, nearly everybody in London realised that something strange was going on. Not only was the air raid alert still in effect, but people going to work could see the Flying Bombs as they shot overhead.

At first sight, they were sinister and frightening – dark, grim-looking things, sputtering flame, making an ominous stuttering-undulating noise. Once in a while, the *duv-duv-duv* would stop suddenly, and the little aircraft dived steeply towards the earth. When it hit, an explosion followed at once; a huge cloud of dark grey smoke marked the place.

Not much work was done on this Friday. With last night's lack of sleep, nobody felt much like working, anyway. The on-and-off alerts kept everyone moving in and out of air raid shelters all day long. Local anti-aircraft batteries added to the nervous strain. The guns kept shooting at the strange aircraft whenever one came within range, dotting the overcast sky with black bursts of shellfire.

Even without all the interruptions, the talk about 'those things' would have brought work to a halt. Rumours flew freely about. Everybody had their own pet theory about the planes, and was more than willing to let everybody and anybody know all about their ideas. Nearly everything was suggested, from 'guided missiles' to 'radio controlled bombers'.

The German High Command made the first official announcement about the Flying Bomb. The news came in a surprisingly low-key statement from Dr Josef Goebbels' Propaganda Ministry. The broadcast simply stated that southern England and the London area were attacked by a new kind of high-explosive missile last night. No mention of 'revenge' was made, at Dr Goebbels' request. There was still no specific news on how much damage was done to London, and Goebbels did not want to raise hopes too high.

Later in the day, the British Government made its own announcement. Herbert Morrison, Minister of Home Security, informed the House of Commons that 'pilotless planes' were being launched against Britain. No mention of London being the target of the 'pilotless planes' was made.

The news media, eager for some word on the new weapon, immediately released the story. 'On the one o'clock news, we were told that the enemy is now using *Pilotless Planes*,' exclaimed Mrs Gwladys Cox, 'and that these had been in action last night during the longest alert of the war ...'

Herbert Morrison's statement did little to ease anyone's mind. If anything, it created even more rumours – 'pilotless plane' could mean anything. 'Radio controlled planes propelled from a shute,' is the way Hilda Neal of South Kensington described the Flying Bombs. 'When they reach a certain distance they discharge their load of bombs and return, still controlled, to base.'

Nor were the rumour-mongers confined to civilians. A friend of US Air Force Sergeant Dick Dudley was dating a young WAAF (Women's Auxiliary Air Force). The young woman informed her friends she had 'inside information' that the pilotless planes were radio controlled.

It was little wonder that people were making up stories about the bombs. A Flying Bomb vibrating overhead at just above rooftop level was a frightening experience – 'an eerie damn feeling' was one man's reaction – more sinister than an attack by a manned bomber. Having some sort of information about them, even if it was made up, was better than having no information at all.

Even the Fire Service was in the dark. In the Official Report for the National Fire Service Region Number 5 (London) for the night of 15th/16th June, the 'incidents' are not given a terribly clear description. Most reports mention only 'Severe damage by explosion and blast.' For two of the explosions, the only explanation offered is 'Enemy action.' The four page account concludes: 'The enemy is reported to be using PAC (Pilotless Aircraft) which appear to cause extensive demolition and blast damage ...'

One concrete fact was known about the bombs: just before a Flying Bomb crashed, its engine would stop abruptly. The heavy *duv-duv-duv* suddenly stopped, and the bomb made its sudden dive.

This 'cutting out' was accidental; the Flying Bomb was meant to come to earth in a power dive. But one thing that the designers of

'The *duv-duv-duv* would stop suddenly, and the little aircraft dove steeply towards the earth.' A Flying Bomb swiftly and silently descends on Central London.

'Thousands of homes in London alone were destroyed.' A Flying Bomb crashed among a group of houses on 2nd July 1944 with this result. Note that there is no crater, but that everything near the point of impact — the white patch in the upper left-hand section, which had been a house — has been demolished.

the *FZG 76* overlooked was a defect in its fuel system. When the windmill device tilted the bomb toward the earth, all the fuel ran to one end of the tank – the end away from the fuel pump. The pump began sucking air and the engine, cut off from its fuel supply, stopped running.

Very quickly people in London and southern England would learn to use the engine's 'cutting out' to their own advantage. Between the time the engine died and the bomb hit the ground, an average of from five to fifteen seconds had passed – ample time to get under some sort of cover. This malfunction in the Flying Bomb undoubtedly saved thousands of lives.

But during the first few days of the Flying Bomb attack, it was just one more inhuman aspect of the sinister machines. A 19-year-old WAAF thought the silence between the cut-off and the explosion was the worst part. To her, it built tension to a nerve-straining crescendo, like the silent interval between movements of a symphony.

For most, the worst part was the constant stream of Alerts, anti-aircraft fire, and All Clears that chased each other through all hours of the day and night. It was normal for the sirens to go any number of times, usually a minimum of six and a maximum of ten or eleven times, every day, for weeks on end.

During Friday night and Saturday and right into Saturday night, the sirens and All Clears followed in rapid succession. Between 4 p.m. on Saturday and 6.30 Sunday morning, the fireguards' log book of an office block in Westminster recorded eleven alerts and All Clears. Some alerts lasted only nine to ten minutes.

People lost track of the sirens; sometimes, it was impossible to tell if there was an alert on or not. This mix-up became the subject of more than one joke. One of the best remembered is a line from a stage-show sketch: a Cockney woman tells her husband, 'I know we must be winning the war. Yesterday I heard 16 Alerts and 24 All Clears.'

Not many saw any humour in the situation. 'Another nasty broken sleep: was awake all night long, with slight intervals of dozing on the bed,' grumbled Hilda Neal in South Kensington. Everybody at Cholmley Gardens, West Hampstead was also kept awake by the constant sirens and periodic anti-aircraft fire.

On Saturday, Mrs Gwladys Cox came across a German propaganda release (not approved by Propaganda Minister Goebbels) that mentioned 'retaliation' against England. 'Goebbels is telling the Germans that "England is trembling!"' Mrs Cox commented. 'England, perhaps I should say southern England, is chiefly sleepy and tired.'

One solution was to go to an air raid shelter, which many people throughout London were doing. 'The shelters in the Underground are crammed again,' Hilda Neal observed. She thought of going down for the night herself, to get away from all the noise and catch some sleep, but finally decided against it.

In the London district of Paddington, the number of occupants in air raid shelters of all types was over 20,000, 5,000 more than in December 1940 during the Blitz. A Paddington Air Raid Warden's log book comments, 'Our Wardens' Service would have an easy time but for the ... allocations of shelterers,' which is 'a bit of a headache for the time being.'

American Intelligence worker Richard Baker's maid told him that she had been forced to stay in her shelter until 5.30 a.m. because of the racket made by the guns. Baker, accustomed to napping in the bathroom, had no trouble at all sleeping.

In spite of the problems caused by the machines, Londoners were soon coining nicknames for them. At first, they were called simply 'pilotless planes' or 'P-Planes'. Residents of the East End called them the 'Farting Furies'. The two most common nicknames were 'buzz bomb' and 'doodlebug', and these were the only names that really stuck.

By midnight of the 16th, seventy-three Flying Bombs had come down on London. Colonel Max Wachtel's *Flakregiment* 155(W) kept launching the bombs at a steady rate. There had been quite a few crashes, but Unteroffizier Otto Neuchel's magic words, 'Go up! Go up!' were still working for him. The worst thing he suffered so far was fatigue. Throughout Saturday, Neuchel kept rolling the Flying Bombs up to his firing ramp at frequent intervals. He doesn't remember how many of the bombs were fired by his battery; he was too busy to keep count.

The *Flakregiment*'s missiles were doing a lot more than just cause sleepless nights. Widespread damage was being done in London, both to war industry and to flats and private homes. Thousands of people had been made homeless – 'bombed out' was the phrase used – and several hundred were killed by the bombs. After an exploding Flying Bomb caused a house or a building to collapse, it was sometimes difficult to tell how many dead and injured were buried until the digging was finished. Reports in log books and Fire Service records frequently mention only 'many killed' or 'heavy casualties'.

In Wood Green, North London, the Tracy family had a very close call, but were far luckier than many. The 17th June was 'an absolutely beautiful summer evening', and was also the first time since the doodlebugs started coming over that they hadn't used their Anderson shelter (an outside shelter, sunk three feet into the back garden and covered by corrugated steel arches).

No one heard the buzz bomb, or realised that it landed – almost on top of the Anderson shelter. When everybody came to, half an hour later, the Air Raid Wardens had arrived and were looking after things. The explosion had turned on all the lights in the house, shattered a solid oak table, but did not injure anyone. About fifty houses including the Tracys' were damaged by the blast. A lot of people were 'filthy dirty', covered by plaster dust and debris, yet not one person was killed.

Colonel Max Wachtel's *Flakregiment* launched its 500th Flying Bomb on Sunday, 18th June. The morning of 18th June was also a particularly hectic one for London's defences and Air Raid Precautions services. In Westminster alone, two major incidents involving Flying Bombs occurred before 9 a.m. The first bomb fell on Hungerford Bridge, the railway bridge across the River Thames to Charing Cross Station.

A gaping hole was blown in the centre of the span, knocking out all access to Charing Cross Station, forcing one of London's major rail terminals to shut down. Later on in the day, Richard Baker of American Intelligence saw the large hole in the bridge, and noticed that several large buildings on the Thames Embankment had all windows facing the river blown out by the explosion.

At 8.35, the second bomb landed among flats in Rutherford Street, about a quarter of a mile south-west of Parliament. The blast from the explosion killed and injured scores of people, caused an outbreak of fire, and partly demolished two five-storey buildings. The Rescue Squad arrived within minutes and began digging dead and wounded out of the rubble.

Each Flying Bomb had an efficient system of sensitive fuses and pressure switches which detonated the warhead at first contact, before the machine could drive itself into the earth. When the 1,900 lbs of high explosives went off right on the surface of a roadway, the blast cut down everything within reach. Solid walls crumbled – often, even individual bricks in a wall were reduced to pebble-sized bits. Windows a quarter of a mile away cracked from the force of the explosion.

When the warhead detonated, shock waves flew out from the explosion within a fraction of a second, moving in concentric circles, like gigantic ripples. As the blast waves pulsed outward, at tremendous speeds, they created a vacuum behind them. This created what one London fireman called a 'double whammy' – the vacuum was capable of creating as much damage as the blast itself.

A Central London fire station got a first-hand, but fortunately harmless, look at the effects of blast from a Flying Bomb. The firemen had the big front doors of the station open, trying to enjoy the sunny but not very warm June day, when a buzz bomb hit less than a block away. With a startling crash, the blast waves slammed the heavy wooden doors shut. A second later the vacuum created by the explosion wrenched them back open again. A man in Bromley, Kent, had a similar experience. He had all his windows open, also trying to get the most out of the summer air, when a doodlebug landed a short distance away. The windows remained intact, but his curtains were sucked '20 yards down the garden'.

Throughout the partly cloudy Sunday morning, local anti-aircraft batteries sporadically opened fire whenever an intruding doodlebug scuttled over, rattling the windows of nearby houses. The flak guns in Hyde Park had been shooting all morning, subjecting the Sunday crowds to their penetrating bang-banging. At about 11.00, a Flying Bomb dodged the flak battery's shell bursts and fell in Bayswater Road, the street running along the Park's northern perimeter. One house was totally destroyed, and several more were severely damaged.

A minute or two later, pedestrians in the vicinity of Victoria

Station heard the loud stuttering noise of an approaching doodlebug. Somewhere over southern Westminster, its persistent *duv-duv-duv* suddenly stopped. Onlookers saw a dark object drop out of the light cloud cover and dive toward the general direction of Parliament. Everyone breathed easier when they saw that the bomb would not hit them, but still kept their eyes on the object, anxious to see where it would come down.

The Chief Air Raid Warden of Westminster, named Charles Norton, saw the bomb hit and explode, but could not tell precisely where it landed – he could only see a 'dense cloud of dust'. He headed toward the cloud, which took him onto Birdcage Walk, the road just south of St James's Park, and saw at once that the Flying Bomb had scored a direct hit on the Guards' Chapel at Wellington Barracks.

Wellington Barracks is the headquarters of the Royal Guards' Division. On this Sunday a special service was being held, which was heavily attended by Guardsmen, both active and retired, and their guests. The bomb struck at a few minutes past eleven o'clock, just after services had started.

It hit the roof of the Chapel, which had been reinforced during the Blitz to withstand incendiary bombs, and apparently managed just to crash through before its warhead went off.

The blast from the near ton of explosives blew the roof away and pulverised the side walls and supporting pillars. 119 people were killed instantly; 141 injured. Only the Bishop of Maidstone was unhurt; he had been giving the service, and was saved by the dome over the altar.

Except for some movement by the altar, the Chief Warden felt a 'ghostly stillness' over the area. One of the survivors of the blast recalls feeling a strange sensation in his ears before the buzz bomb struck. This sensation became a 'loud, horrible buzzing' that, at what must have been the moment of explosion, turned into a high-pitched whine. After that, everything went dark, and he heard a woman with a high-pitched voice singing 'The Rose of Tralee'. The next thing he remembers is being lifted out of the rubble by the Rescue Squad.

Civil Defence Rescue Workers kept pulling the wounded and dead out of the debris, with the help of cranes, for forty-eight hours.

A sizable crowd gathered in Birdcage Walk to watch the grim business, and to gape at the wreckage of the Chapel. The large, solid building looked as though it had been cut in half horizontally, with the top half missing. Nothing could have made plainer the incredible damage that could be done by the pilotless planes.

London newspapers hardly mentioned the incident. The *News Chronicle* reported only that 'A church in south England' was hit by a 'P-Plane' in Monday the 19th's edition. But it did not take much imagination to see the implications. Only a short walk from the Guards' Chapel was Whitehall and the nerve centre of Britain's war effort – Intelligence Headquarters; Downing Street; Parliament.

The very day after the incident, Winston Churchill ordered that the House of Commons be evacuated to Church House, just as he had done in November 1940, at the height of the Blitz. Church House, a modern steel structure and far more substantial than the House of Commons, lies about three hundred yards west of Parliament. The transfer to the new quarters began at once.

Even though Church House was only a short distance away, moving involved a lot of bother and re-arranging. Churchill's order did not sit well with everyone. Shortly after the transfer was made, one Member of Parliament demanded to know why they had to come back. Before Winston Churchill could answer, another Member spoke up. He invited the first man to walk a few hundred yards over to Birdcage Walk, where he would see the reason for himself. Nothing more had to be said.

An even more immediate and far-reaching result of the Guards' Chapel incident took place that same afternoon. General Dwight D. Eisenhower made a ruling that air attacks on Flying Bomb sites in France would now have precedence over all else, except for the most urgent requirements of the battle in Normandy.

General Eisenhower's order diverted over thirty per cent of RAF and US Army Air Force bomber strikes away from industrial targets inside Germany. As expected, the order was not very popular among Allied bombing commanders.

General Carl 'Tooey' Spaatz, Commander of American Army Air Forces, suggested air raids on German factories that made the gyro-mechanisms for the Flying Bombs. In a strongly worded letter to General Eisenhower, General Spaatz pointed out that bomber operations over Germany were the surest and swiftest means of ending German resistance, and should have 'overruling priority'. But Eisenhower's order stood despite all objections.

One of Adolf Hitler's main objectives in launching the Flying Bomb assault was to divert Allied bombers away from German cities. Hitler hoped that Allied commanders would begin attacking the launch sites, leaving fewer bombers to attack industrial centres in the Ruhr Valley and other areas throughout Germany. He had already achieved one of his primary goals, and the Flying Bomb attack was not even a week old.

Another order issued on 18th June had nothing whatever to do with the Flying Bomb on the Guards' Chapel. This was the decision by Anti-Aircraft Command that flak guns inside London would no longer be allowed to shoot at buzz bombs over the city. Once a bomb got inside London's defences it would be allowed to fly on, where, hopefully, it would crash in the open countryside to the north.

Anti-aircraft gunners had been shooting at every doodlebug within range – and, with practice, managed to hit a few – thinking that the bombs would explode harmlessly in mid-air. But everyone found out very quickly that this was not true at all.

When caught by a flak burst, a Flying Bomb behaved like any conventional aircraft – it lost altitude rapidly and crashed into the ground. Occasionally, a shell would explode the warhead, sending bits of the demolished buzz bomb flying for miles in all directions. But usually the bomb's delicate control mechanism was the first thing to go, making the machine veer earthward, out of control.

It made no difference, everyone soon learned whether a buzz bomb fell to earth by itself or with the help of anti-aircraft fire – it still had the same devastating effect.

So far fourteen doodlebugs had been shot down by the anti-aircraft guns. Eleven fell in built-up areas of London, destroying property and slowing down war production. An eyewitness recalls, 'Each explosion was accompanied by a huge burst of red fire that lit up the sky with a transient rosy glow.' From the 18th onward, gunners were forbidden to shoot at Flying Bombs inside the Greater London region.

The reasoning behind the sudden cease-fire was sound enough, but it did not help London's shaky morale. After the guns gave the buzz bombs the 'silent treatment' – the GI expression – letters from residents of all London boroughs began pouring in to police stations, newspapers, Members of Parliament and even Winston Churchill. Some of the letters were angry, others were merely curious, but they all wanted to know why the flak batteries had stopped firing back at the Flying Bombs.

This was another throwback to the Blitz. During the night-time raids of 1940 and 1941, the guns rarely brought down a Luftwaffe raider. But people were given a sense of 'hitting back' by the ear-shattering *bang-bang-banging* of the guns. Even though it cost them a night's sleep, Londoners were reassured by the shattering noise.

Winston Churchill's War Cabinet had enough to worry about without thinking of civilian complaints. On 19th June, Duncan Sandys was appointed by Churchill as Chairman of the Flying Bomb Defence Committee; his official title was Chairman of the War Cabinet Committee on Operational Counter-Measures Against the Flying Bomb. Sandys had been out of the picture for seven months, but had kept up his reading of intelligence reports on enemy activities. Now he was back to coordinate the attack against the robot bombs.

Duncan Sandys' new job was a complex one, but reorganising the defences had already begun. After prohibiting gunners to fire on buzz bombs over London, General Sir Frederick Pile, the chief of Anti-Aircraft Command, had begun moving his flak batteries to the North Downs, about thirty miles in from the coast. Hundreds of guns from all over Britain were moved to a seventy mile stretch of Kent and Sussex. All Flying Bombs launched from the Pas de Calais would have to fly over this 'gun belt' on their way to London.

Also, 1,000 barrage balloons were shifted to a position south-east of London, another barrier for the Flying Bombs. In London and throughout the Home Counties, the most widely heard comment about the local balloons was that they 'disappeared overnight' during this move.

By 21st June, all barrage balloons and nearly all guns were in position. Also, eight fighter squadrons were flying standing patrols at 6,000 feet; 'scrambling' took too much time. The squadrons assigned to deal with the doodlebugs were equipped with fast-flying

Tempest Vs, Spitfire IXs and XIVs, and Hawker Typhoons.

Fighters were able to overtake the slower buzz bombs – the speed of a Flying Bomb varied from machine to machine, from 300 to 450 mph – and could shoot them down like a conventional aeroplane. Several of the bombs had already been disposed of by Spitfires. The first was shot down just after midnight on 16th June.

All the elements were in place, but the complications were only beginning. One of the main difficulties was with the anti-aircraft guns and their problems in tracking the low-flying buzz bombs. The Flying Bombs had been reported to zoom along at 6,000 or 7,000 feet, but actually they flew at 2,000 to 3,000 feet, and sometimes lower. Hand-controlled 20 mm and 40 mm guns could not traverse fast enough to keep up with the fast and low buzz bombs.

So it became necessary to bring in the heavy 3.7-inch static guns, which traversed and elevated mechanically. But these guns required concrete platforms as foundations. Pouring all the concrete for over three hundred 3.7-inch guns would take months.

Within a matter of days, however, this problem was solved. Instead of a concrete base, a pre-manufactured foundation was installed. This platform, christened the 'Pile Mattress', could be brought up, anchored to the ground, and mounted with a 3.7-inch gun within hours. They were being installed before the end of June.

With one piece of bad news out of the way, it didn't take long for another to crop up. Now, the problem was between the anti-aircraft guns and the patrolling fighter screen.

Fighter pilots complained that the anti-aircraft fire made it impossible to pursue a doodlebug – pilots had a healthy distrust of *any* flak gunners, and felt that the 'friendly' shell bursts had as good a chance of hitting them as of wiping out any buzz bomb.

The gunners complained that the fighters kept flying within range of their guns – the pilots had no business entering their territory. When patrolling Spitfires and Tempests began coming back to base showing ragged holes from anti-aircraft shell splinters, the controversy started to heat up. Something had to be done.

In order to avoid a full-scale mutiny, Anti-Aircraft Command and the RAF drew up a maddeningly complex list of rules and regulations on combating the Flying Bomb. Most pilots and gunners couldn't even remember them, much less stick to them.

Fighters and anti-aircraft, according to the rules, were not permitted to operate together. Fighters could not enter a gun zone unless actually pursuing a buzz bomb. Guns were not allowed to fire when fighters were operating. On a clear day, the guns were not allowed to fire at all, but when it was cloudy the flak batteries were free to fire on their own. If a fighter entered the anti-aircraft zone, it was up to the gunners to recognise a friendly aircraft from a doodlebug and cease firing. The way it turned out, nobody was happy; all parties wound up frustrated and confused.

One by one, the problems were being ironed out, slowly but surely. At the end of June, the Control Room at Stanmore, Middlesex, was plotting an average of 100 bombs per day on its great map of England. The defenders were getting a large percentage of them – fighters were bringing down about thirty per day; balloons accounted for between eight and ten – and some were overflying the capital. But an average of fifty Flying Bombs were hitting London every twenty-four hours.

By 27th June, two weeks after the first Flying Bomb fell on Gravesend, Kent, just under 2,000 people had been killed by the bombs. Thousands of homes in London alone had been destroyed, uprooting the lives of countless people. Production in London factories dropped dramatically. More than 16% of each work week had been lost because of the attacks – especially noteworthy since 40% of Britain's 1,000-lb high explosive bombs, the type used against targets in Germany, came out of London factories. Much of the time lost was due to the constant Alerts, which kept workers in the shelters an average of one working day every week.

Government restrictions forced newspapers to play down the effects of the Flying Bomb, and reporters were prohibited from mentioning London in their stories – they were only allowed to say that 'southern England' was under attack. The penalty for violating the strict censorship law was a heavy fine, and a possible prison sentence, on charges of 'supplying useful information to the enemy'.

Most news stories were not very informative. Some were totally misleading. BBC correspondent A.P. Ryan reported, 'Neither casualties nor damage have been very heavy, and the various counter-measures are doing well,' and adds. 'The things do only reach the south of England.'

Southern England includes London, and the facts were not nearly as optimistic as A.P. Ryan's broadcast.

Damage to targets of military importance – factories, railways, communication centres – were also nothing to be shrugged off. On the same day that the Guards' Chapel was destroyed, no fewer than eleven factories were hit by buzz bombs. The 'essential war services' were also thrown into a turmoil. Four telephone exchanges had been destroyed or badly damaged; gas supplies, water supplies, and electricity were cut off to various sections of London; and several hospitals had been hit and evacuated. On top of this, seven railway stations, including Victoria, London Bridge, and Charing Cross had been closed because of bomb damage.

The Flying Bombs were also having another effect, less visible but just as harmful. The appearance of the buzz bombs so shortly after D-Day came as a nasty blow to London's morale.

In the backs of their minds, most people had a secret belief that the landings in France would signal some instant, miraculous change in the war. The enemy would somehow collapse and the war would come to a swift, breathtaking finish, if not this month, then surely by the end of summer. Instead, there was a return to the anxiety of 1940 – air raid sirens, shelters, sleepless nights, and sudden explosions.

Especially during the first two weeks of the pilotless attacks, conversation centred on the new machines. Neighbours often spoke about the machines in hushed tones, as though mentioning the planes out loud might bring one down on top of them. Men and women alike had a genuine fear of the Flying Bombs. Richard Baker of American Intelligence was stopped on the street one day by an Indian, a complete stranger, who nervously told Baker how horrible and diabolic he thought the machines were. A girl who lived in Bethnal Green, East London, recalls, 'The Flying Bombs were the terror of our lives ... we sat under the table with our hearts in our mouths until the dreadful explosion came ...'

Along with the pilotless planes, the fighting in Normandy was another cause for anxiety. The expected push toward Germany had bogged down in what General Dwight D. Eisenhower called 'The

Battle of the Beachhead', hard, heavy fighting but little or no gains in enemy-held territory.

Much of the fighting took place near Caen, an important objective that the German army stubbornly defended. So far, the Wehrmacht had stopped dead the Allied advance. Some resistance had been expected, but not this kind of drawn-out slugging.

Just about everyone in southern England had seen evidence of the massive D-Day build-up; the hordes of uniforms and Jeeps and staff cars in London's streets was proof enough. The size of the operation alone inspired confidence, giving the impression that its success was a foregone conclusion. But now the Germans were turning back everything the British, Americans, and Canadians threw at them, and showed no signs of tiring.

Veterans of the First World War remembered Gallipoli, the combined British and French landings on the beaches of Turkey in 1915. The landings at Gallipoli were aimed at capturing the Dardanelles and the Turkish capital of Constantinople, and were intended to have a profound effect on the First World War's outcome. But the Gallipoli campaign turned into a drawn-out battle of attrition, and a steady drain on French and British resources. Eleven months later, the Allied troops were withdrawn. The invasion was a failure.

Nearly three weeks after D-Day, on 26th June 1944, the port of Cherbourg was captured, giving the invading armies a base for unloading supplies. But the final, dramatic climax that everyone hoped for did not take place. The Battle of the Beachhead dragged on, with only slight, local gains inland from the Normandy beaches.

For London, the battle 'across the Channel' was something that was read about with great concern in *The Times* or the *Mirror*. The Flying Bombs, trundling overhead both day and night, were a more immediate worry.

The Flying Bomb assault was now being referred to as 'The Second Battle of London'. It was only natural for residents of the British capital to compare it to the First Battle of London, the Blitz of 1940 and 1941.

American Intelligence worker Richard Baker was told by a friend, a resident of London, that the buzz bombs were different from the Luftwaffe bombers of nearly four years before. During the Blitz, everybody just clenched their teeth and tried to carry on. Now, everybody seemed much more skittish and jumpy. The strain was also making everyone nastier and short-tempered.

A young fellow in St John's Wood named Dennis Horsford was more outspoken. The doodlebugs gave him a special kind of frustration. When a buzz bomb was brought down, there was none of the 'vindictive satisfaction' of knowing that the plane had several Germans inside it. 'Back in the days of the Blitz, a fallen Heinkel was full of the bastards who were trying to kill you!'

Because the buzz bombs had no pilot, a series of strange, super-natural tales began to circulate about them. This simple, unsophisticated jet-propelled torpedo has been credited with some of the most amazing of feats.

The most common thought was that the doodlebugs actually had the power of seeking out and pursuing its victims – a young woman thought that a Flying Bomb once chased her the length of Harley Street. Others 'knew' that buzz bombs were zeroed in on a certain district, and that 'they circled round and round' until they found their target. An American airman on leave in Dover caught sight of a procession of Flying Bombs on their way over from France. More than 35 years later he recalls: 'We swore they were flying in formation.'

There was no real relief from the Flying Bombs. Unlike the Luftwaffe's bomber fleets, the buzz bombs came over during daylight hours and during cloudy and rainy weather. Even so, London was gradually learning to live with the threat. People soon realised that as long as the thing kept going, making its loud, rattling *duv-duv-duv* noise, they were all right. If the bomb's engine should suddenly cut out, the thing to do was get under a table or leave the room and go out in the hall – away from glass – until the *booomm*!

After the anti-aircraft guns had been pulled out of London, ending the danger of being hit by shrapnel from bursting anti-aircraft shells, there was even the temptation to go out and have a look at a real, in-the-flesh doodlebug.

American Army Air Force officer Truman Smith, a B-17 Flying Fortress pilot in the 385th Bomb Group (H), was in a London tailor's shop one day to have his uniform altered. When the air raid Alert sounded, everyone in the shop, staff and customers, went out into the street to watch the buzz bomb fly over, and Smith followed along. He was in London on a 48-hour pass; at his base, he had been warned about the doodlebugs and wanted to catch a glimpse of one.

From the middle of the street everyone scanned the sky, looking for the bomb. An electric alarm bell went off somewhere, and Smith heard an Air Raid Warden blowing a whistle – warnings that a buzz bomb was in the area.

The Flying Bomb came within earshot a few moments later, 'a terrible sounding thing ... unique ... an ominous sound all its own.' Now everybody really strained to see the approaching bomb. The sound of the engine grew louder and louder and suddenly – stopped.

Smith became aware of an eerie silence, 'not even traffic sounds,' but continued his look-out for the bomb just the same. Something made him bring his eyes down to street level, when he got a very sharp surprise. There was nobody in sight. The street was completely empty, except for him, standing in the middle of it.

It didn't take long for him to collect his thoughts. He ran back into the shop, where he was hailed to join the crowd under the tailor's table. He got to the table at about the same time as the doodlebug exploded a few blocks away. From there he was in no position to observe anything, and remembers, 'I didn't get to see that one.' But there would be other chances in the months to come.

Watching for the bombs was now a regular pastime. People watched from the street, from rooftops, from sitting room windows. It wasn't just to keep an eye out for danger, but was frequently motivated by nothing more than simple curiosity. 'I watch them sailing along from my bedroom window,' Mrs Gwladys Cox recounts from her flat in Hampstead, 'a curious sight, like a will-o'-the-wisp in the night'. Between midnight and 2 a.m. one morning, Mrs Cox counted the flaming jets of eighteen doodlebugs passing over.

There were plenty of doodlebugs to see, more every day. By the end of June, close to 800 Flying Bombs had hit London, and an average of about fifty were still landing on the capital every day.

'The day longed for by 80 million Germans has come.' An announcement of the Third Reich's revenge appeared, without Josef Goebbels' approval, in the 20th June edition of the newspaper *Berliner Nachtausgabe*. This article greatly angered and upset Propaganda Minister Goebbels. He had expressly forbidden the words 'revenge' or 'retaliation' in radio and press releases – he had his doubts about the Flying Bomb, and was afraid the German public might be misled into believing that the machines could win the war. So incensed was Goebbels that he threatened to have the reporter who wrote the article shot.

But the word had got out, and other news sources followed the *Berliner Nachtausgabe* article. Within a few days, the new Flying Bomb was being spoken of as a vengeance weapon. So Goebbels had no choice but to make an official announcement himself. On the 24th, he coined the term *Vergeltungswaffe 1* (V-1) implying that there would be more secret weapons to come.

Civilian morale was given a brief lift by the announcement. For months, everyone had been told to 'keep a stout and valiant heart', and they were tired of hearing it. Now, at least there was something concrete to pin their hopes on.

A letter written by a German civilian to a soldier in Normandy exclaims, 'The whole of Germany is now occupied with the two latest events: the invasion and the new weapon.' Another declares, 'At last, our revenge against England has begun,' and a third letter writer wonders, 'when will V-2 be due?'

Berlin, Hamburg, and other heavily bombed cities welcomed the *Wunderwaffen* with great excitement. But some doubts were already beginning to creep into some conversations. A letter dated 21st June fears that the British and Americans 'are not going to take all that lying down,' and that Allied air strikes might get worse because of the Flying Bombs. The V-1 won't win the war, only antagonise the enemy.

These fears were more than justified. On the night of 21st June, Berlin was pounded by its heaviest air raid to date in direct retaliation for the V-1s. Twenty-five hundred RAF bombers toggled their loads of high explosives over the city that night. On the next day, 22nd June, 1,000 USAAF bombers, escorted by 1,200 fighters, started large fires in the German capital and caused heavy damage.

The Swedish newspaper *Morgon Tidningen* reported from Berlin that heavy clouds of smoke hung over the city, hiding the sun from view. At 11 a.m. the smoke made the bright late morning sky 'like twilight'.

Adolf Hitler's confidence in the V-1 could not be shaken by an Allied air raid, no matter how heavy. He was delighted to be hitting back at England again. Hitler hoped that the Flying Bombs would turn the war back to 1940, and that his new weapons would do what the Luftwaffe couldn't – break Britain's will to carry on the fight.

General Erich Heinemann and other high ranking officers assured Hitler that the Flying Bombs were enjoying a huge success, but that these attacks could not continue unless production of the V-1 was stepped up. Firing only 100 bombs a day at London would have no real effect. The launching crews needed more Flying Bombs and more supplies if the attack was to continue.

The point was well taken by Hitler. He wanted London pounded round the clock by the Flying Bombs which, according to reports from all sides, were doing an outstanding job. But to increase production of the V-1s, work on something else, some other project, would have to be cut back.

All reports on the A-4 long-range rocket were just the opposite of the Flying Bomb accounts. Experiments were still going on, but no real progress was being made. In spite of months of tests and more tests, the rockets still blew up in mid-air, or else went haywire soon after launching.

Wernher von Braun and General Walter Dornberger reported that their A-4 was still having problems, but there was nothing that couldn't be solved. To Hitler, however, the rockets were only a possibility, while the V-1 was already paying off.

At Berchtesgaden in late June, Hitler came to a decision regarding the two weapons. The V-1 Flying Bomb would have its production increased, while the A-4 rocket would be cut back. Whatever manpower and materials were needed to step up the V-1 would be taken from the A-4 project.

The A4 rocket still gave its designers fits of depression, but never despair. At Blinza, in Poland and on the rail line with the gigantic underground rocket factory at Nordhausen, the bugs that infested the A-4 were being worked out with agonising slowness.

Almost constant changes in the rocket's unimaginably complex workings kept production at a snail's pace. The great Nordhausen works, in Central Germany's Hartz Mountains, was actually capable of building nearly 700 A-4 rockets every month. But literally thousands of changes had been made in the rocket so far, and more were still pouring in. Every time a modification was called for, a new set of blueprints had to be drawn up, new jigs and dies had to be made – all time-consuming and frustrating.

The most stubborn difficulty was the 'air burst' problem – the launch would go according to plan, but the rocket mysteriously exploded several thousand feet in the air. In March 1944, only four of twenty-six successfully launched A-4s did not end their flight in a blossom of smoke. Everybody had their own theory of what was at the root of the problem: faulty electrical systems; careless launch crews. General Dornberger believed that the liquid oxygen tank was exploding, while Wernher von Braun thought it was the alcohol tank.

Along with the scientists and technicians, the launching units that would fire the A-4 at enemy targets had also moved to Blinza. There were three outfits, each having names that sounded like nothing more than conventional artillery units: 836 (Mobile) Artillery Detachment; 444 (Training and Experimental) Battery; 485 (Mobile) Artillery Detachment.

Simple firing tables were being used by the field units, replacing the elaborate test stands that had been used at Peenemünde. The small, cone-shaped platforms, usually described as resembling lemon squeezers, had one huge advantage over the Peenemünde test stands – mobility.

These launching tables could be set down on any level stretch of ground – a clearing in a forest or even the middle of a roadway – to support the rocket launch, and be whisked away before patrolling Allied fighter-bombers could find it.

All the launching crews were fully trained and ready for actual operations by June 1944. All they needed were rockets that worked. Most of the A-4s they launched blew up high overhead, strewing chunks of rocket parts all round. The men in the firing detachments felt like Prom Queens in a one-horse town – all dressed up with nowhere to go.

CHAPTER FOUR

'Keep ... Firing With All Dispatch'

Phil Haring, manager of the Gentleman's Hairdressing Salon in Bush House, recalls that there had been 'a heck of a lot' of buzz bombs on the morning of 30th June – not a very precise estimate, but right enough. By early afternoon, 38 Flying Bombs had crash-dived into London, and the city had been under constant alert since just after 7 a.m. It was an unusually warm, clear day for this cool and rainy summer; from rooftops and high office windows, the bombs could be spotted while still miles away as they trundled up from the south.

Bush House, a huge office complex in the crescent-shaped street called the Aldwych, just off Central London's Strand, had an observer's post on the roof and an air raid shelter in the basement. Every time a doodlebug came in sight, the Royal Observers would sound the local Alert. But except for a handful of nervous office girls who practically lived in the shelter, hardly anybody paid any attention to the persistent alarms – there were too many to bother about.

Just before 2 p.m., one of the bombs abruptly cut out somewhere over Waterloo Station. American Intelligence worker Richard Baker heard the engine stop and made a dive for the corridor, trying to get away from the windows. Before he could take more than a few steps Baker was thrown to the floor, along with bits of broken glass and chunks of plaster from the walls and ceiling. He heard the explosion and felt the blast as he fell, but, apart from being blown off balance, knew he was all right.

Richard Baker was far more fortunate than many. The Flying Bomb had gone into a sharp, almost vertical, dive, and struck near the main door of the Air Ministry building, across the Aldwych from Bush House. Scores of people were out on the street, on their lunch hour, when the bomb landed.

A staff member of the British Broadcasting Company in Bush House saw an 'enormous black cloud' directly after the explosion. Ten yards from the blasted-out window, he saw the body of a man who had been killed outright by the explosion. All around were cut and bleeding men and women, some lying still, some sitting on the pavement, others wandering about with glassy expressions.

Inside the Air Ministry Building the walls seemed to arch and bend like rubber, and windows bowed first inward and then outward by the force of the blast. For those who heard the warning and braced themselves, the explosion still came as an unpleasant jolt – the close, intense burst jarred even the rock-solid buildings along the Aldwych.

More than one hundred lives were wiped out in an instant. To some, it seemed as though the bomb could reach out and choose its victims. An Air Force officer saw the man standing next to him chopped to shreds by slivers of flying glass, which hit with the force of a shotgun burst, while he himself suffered only minor cuts. A young WAAF was lifted off her feet by the concussion. She regained consciousness and discovered that the other girls with her had all been killed.

Several other WAAFs died under more bizarre circumstances. They had been standing by an open window, leaning halfway out to get a look at the passing buzz bomb, when it dived into the Aldwych. The same vicious shock waves that bent window panes outward sucked the blue uniformed women out through the open window. On the pavement below, their faces reflected their last astonished expressions.

In his hairdressing salon in Bush House, Phil Haring didn't hear the Flying Bomb approach. The first he knew of the bomb was when he felt 'a sort of thud'; then all the lights went off for a few seconds and came back on again. Just about every piece of glass in the shop was shattered by the blast – all the mirrors broke, so did a glass cabinet – and the light globes fell from the ceiling.

Haring's first thought was for his customers and staff. But a quick check told him that no one had been hurt, even though the inside of his salon was a mess of broken glass. As a former member of the Royal Army Medical Corps, Haring had a good background in First Aid and treatment. So, after making sure of his own clients and employees, he went out into the Aldwych to see what he could do.

The first thing that met his eyes was the heavy layer of rubble and broken glass, and the number of bodies – the ground was 'saturated with bodies'. Dead and injured 'in any imaginable position' were strewn all about. Some were half-buried under piles of fallen masonry or parts from a blasted-out bus. Others sat on the ground, cut and bleeding, in a state of dazed bewilderment.

Phil Haring made his way across the street to the Post Office, which had been doing a brisk business when the bomb landed. There were still people alive in there; all Haring could hear was a steady chorus of moaning from the injured. Later, he would find out that a girl from a nearby office had gone into the Post Office on an errand just before the explosion. No trace of her was ever found. She had, Haring supposes, 'gone to dust', blown away by the Flying Bomb's awesome blast.

Civil Defence Services were quickly on the scene: the Rescue Squad, to reach persons trapped in the debris; First Aid Squad, Police and Medical Services, Fire Service, Home Guard and local clergymen, and even US Army personnel with Jeeps.

Phil Haring stayed out in the street with the rescue services for the next 'two or three hours', helping to look after the wounded. There were so many bodies, dead and living, that no time could be spent on formalities. The first thing done was to feel the victim's pulse; if the person was dead, he was covered with a cloth and the next one was tended to.

Army vehicles arrived soon afterward and began a shuttle service, taking the wounded to hospitals and coming back for more. Hilda Neal of South Kensington watched ambulances and vans 'tearing backwards and forwards' to and from Charing Cross Hospital, about a half mile down the Strand from the explosion, and could see the injured lying on the floors of the vehicles.

There were so many casualties that all the local hospitals were soon full. Charing Cross, St Bartholomew's, and Westminster Hospital quickly ran out of room. Not knowing what else to do, ambulance drivers took the stretcher cases to any sheltered area

The Aldwych Flying Bomb Incident

'The Flying Bomb ... struck near the main door of the Air Ministry building ...' After the explosion, the Air Ministry Building shows the scars of the bomb's impact.

'More than one hundred lives were wiped out in an instant.' A victim of the explosion lies where he fell, half-buried under a part from a blasted-out vehicle. Note the expressions of the onlookers.

close by, including railway arches.

While all this activity was going on, the restaurant next door to Phil Haring's salon quietly did its bit by giving free tea and sandwiches to the police and rescue men. Outside, the Fire Service hosed down the pavement to wash away the blood.

When the final numbers were in, the total killed was put at 198 persons; hundreds more were injured. The term 'injured' could mean anything, however, from an amputated arm or leg to a minor flesh wound.

Richard Baker had no idea that he had been hurt until someone told him. He had been hit in the neck by glass and was bleeding fairly freely. After a while, he felt the warm trickle of blood oozing down his side. He walked to a nearby First Aid centre on the Strand, where his wound was cleaned and dressed. Afterwards, Baker admitted that he felt like a minor hero.

Not every injury could be counted on the official lists, for not all were physical. It would take many people weeks or months to get over the shock of seeing violent death at such close quarters. Some would never get over it.

A female co-worker of Richard Baker's, though unhurt, was frightened to the point of not being able to move. She clung to Baker, sobbing, for some time after the explosion. One of the 'nervous office girls' who hadn't gone to shelter watched as her friend from the office next door was killed outright by the bomb's concussion. Her own injuries included partial loss of vision in one eye and many deep cuts. She was also unable to speak. Even weeks after her wounds had healed, she still could not make any vocal sounds at all. During the next ten years, she would undergo two complete breakdowns and, thirty-five years later, still suffered from a chronic nervous disorder.

'Everybody in my crew worked like damn hell, including me,' Unteroffizier Otto Neuchel emphasised. 'Our officers told us, "Keep the catapults firing with all dispatch," and we did. Only none of us knew where our bombs were going. We just rolled them up ... and watched them go up. After they left the ramp, we didn't know what happened.'

Unteroffizier Neuchel and his men weren't the only ones. Neither

Colonel Max Wachtel, Colonel Wachtel's superiors, nor the German High Command had any accurate knowledge of where the Flying Bombs were coming down.

Reconnaissance flights over London were almost non-existent. During the Blitz, camera equipped aircraft made regular sorties over the British capital, taking sharp, clear photos of the damage done by the Luftwaffe's night bombing raids. But since 1941, things had changed drastically. Allied fighters made photographing London a hazardous, if not altogether impossible, assignment.

A few reconnaissance planes did manage to overfly London at night. The pilot of one flight gave a vivid account of fires he had seen burning during the early hours of 16th June, which appeared in a weekly propaganda publication. But no Luftwaffe camera planes got over by day.

Germany's intelligence network was not what it had been in 1941, either. During the Blitz, the Luftwaffe High Command had been supplied with a good deal of invaluable information by neutral journalists. British reporters were not allowed to mention any specific locations or details, which made for bland and not very exciting news stories. But on the day after a big raid, Swedish papers carried full particulars of bomb damage in London, naming districts, street addresses, and even individual buildings.

In the summer of 1944, however, the war was clearly not going well for Germany. Little pressure could be brought to bear on neutral countries. Besides, the neutrals did not want to be caught supporting the wrong side when the war ended. Helpful reports from Swedish newspapers had all but petered out.

German Intelligence and the Luftwaffe knew that the V-1 Flying Bombs were landing on and around London – nothing could miss a hundred square-mile target – but did not know exactly where. After a Flying Bomb knocked out Hungerford Bridge on 18th June, German agents in London got the message through, but the report somehow became confused. The bomb was first reported to have hit Hungerford Bridge. A few days later, the report was changed to 'Hungerford, London' and later became 'Hungerford-near-London.'

On 6th July, Winston Churchill gave a report on the Flying Bomb in a speech to the House of Commons, mentioning 'London' and 'Greater London' several times – the first time anyone officially admitted that London was being hit by the pilotless machines. Churchill also admitted that he was being 'very careful to be vague about areas ...'

But Britain was unwittingly supplying the enemy with information right in the pages of London newspapers. In reporting the deaths of Londoners killed by the pilotless planes, obituary columns ran notices that included the phrase, 'As the result of enemy action ...' – a giveaway to any sharp-eyed German agent.

The obituary listings of *The Times* and *The Telegraph* ran several 'enemy action' notices in each edition, complete with full addresses, giving the enemy all details. In the 6th July edition of *The Times*, this death notice appeared: died 'As the result of enemy action, Cecil Vivian Moore of 3 Avonmore Road, West Kensington, W14 ...' British Intelligence eventually caught on and put a stop to it, but not before much useful data leaked over to the 'other side'.

Shortly after the Flying Bomb attack began, British Intelligence decided to trick the German agents with their own system. The scientific liaison officer attached to British Intelligence, Dr R.V. Jones, came up with an idea for feeding the enemy false information and spoiling the aim of Colonel Max Wachtel's *Flakregiment*.

The Intelligence services had a number of 'controlled' agents working for them – agents specially trained to feed phoney, but authentic-sounding, information to the enemy. It would require a bit of calculating, but it should pose no special problem for the controlled agents to pass along the wrong position each time a Flying Bomb came down on London.

The plan was to give Colonel Wachtel a mistaken impression of where he was sending his pilotless planes, making Wachtel re-adjust his bombs so that they would fall south of the River Thames, far short of their aiming point. So, when Flying Bombs landed on Central London, the controlled agents reported that the bombs had overshot their mark and landed in the countryside to the north. If the machines came down south of the Thames, the agents would send back a report that Central London was being badly shaken.

By the end of June, Colonel Wachtel and his superiors received word from 'reliable' sources that Central London was hard hit, and that no Flying Bombs had landed south of the Thames. Actually, three-quarters of the bombs had come down on the southern side of the river.

It was a sly trick, but it worked. A few days afterwards, Colonel Wachtel's crews began re-adjusting the Flying Bombs' guidance mechanisms. In London the great, jarring explosions began marching farther and farther south; the point of impact was changed from Tower Bridge to Dulwich, about five miles to the south. This was fine for those living in Central districts, like Westminster and Chelsea, but cold comfort to residents of southern regions like Croydon, which suffered more Flying Bomb damage than any other area.

While Intelligence was doing its best to hoax the Germans, the Luftwaffe was pulling a few less subtle tricks of its own. Flying Bombs were now being fitted with cable-cutting wing edges, knife-like steel attachments bolted to the leading edges of the wings. These were designed to cut through the cables of the barrage balloon screen that protected London's southern boundary, and they did the job to perfection. Whizzing through the air at about 400 mph, the blades chopped right through the balloon cables. By September, over 600 balloons were cut adrift from the protective shield.

Also, a new explosive was being tried out. Flying Bomb warheads were being filled with Trialen, an aluminium explosive with twice the blast-effect of TNT. The Trialen warheads also contained more of the new explosive: 2,031 lbs, compared with 1,870 of the conventional filler. Three days after the Aldwych incident, a Flying Bomb landed on Turks Row, Chelsea. One hundred and twenty-four people died in the blast.

After the anti-aircraft guns moved to the North Downs, the total of buzz bombs destroyed by the defences had improved. Flak gunners were shooting down an increasing number of machines. But in early July, most of the Flying Bombs were still being brought down by fighters.

'It's like firing at a large flame with wings sprouting out of it,' recounted a Tempest V pilot of an attack on a buzz bomb. 'Your cannon scores hits, and suddenly there is a big red flash ...'

The top doodlebug 'ace' was Squadron Leader Joseph Berry,

who also flew a Tempest. Berry's final score was $61\frac{1}{3}$ kills: 57 were shot down at night; $4\frac{1}{3}$ in the daytime. He got his $\frac{1}{3}$ of a doodlebug on a day patrol when he pursued a machine over the gun belt. His Tempest's machine gun fire first hit the Flying Bomb, which then ran into an anti-aircraft burst and finally struck a barrage balloon cable before crashing. Each unit was credited with one-third of the buzz bomb.

Number 616 Squadron's jet-propelled Gloster Meteor fighters could combat the pilotless planes on an equal footing. The Meteor had a maximum speed of well over 400 mph, and would account for 13 Flying Bombs when the squadron became operational in August. But the most frequently used fighter continued to be the Tempest V and Spitfire XIV.

Fighters assigned to 'Diver' operations underwent careful and exacting modifications to squeeze every last bit of speed from their powerplants. All armour and excess weight was removed. Leading edges of wings and stabilisers were polished to a high gloss. The engines themselves received particular care – meticulous tuning and overhauling. After all the cutting and streamlining, the Flying Bomb interceptors consisted of little more than machine guns and cannon, a fuel tank, and a finely-tuned engine.

Pilots of the modified Spitfires and Tempests were now able to close with the doodlebugs a bit more easily. Some could even pull right alongside the less speedy machines, close enough to read the German writing on the fuselage. A few enterprising flyers discovered that they could slide one wing under the wing of the 'flying blowlamp' and execute a roll, flipping the Flying Bomb over and out of control. This quickly became a standard method of destroying the bombs, known as 'tipping'.

'Tipping the doodlebugs' nearly always worked. The Flying Bomb had a very sensitive and delicate gyro mechanism; any sudden, violent movements, such as wing-lifting, would upset the gyro, causing it to malfunction. With its gyroscope out of order, the machine tumbled earthward in a crazy spin. From the air, the concentric shock wave of the crashed bomb looked like 'a single ripple on a lake'.

But this manoeuvre was not without its risks. The Flying Bombs were made of rolled sheet steel, while the RAF fighters had a skin of

'It's like firing at a large flame with wings sprouting out of it.' Above the green countryside south of London, a 'Diver Patrol' Spitfire tries to close with a Flying Bomb (in circle). The Spitfire, marked with black and white D-Day 'Invasion Stripes', is still well beyond machine-gun range.

light aluminium alloy. Many a Spitfire and Tempest hobbled back to its landing field with one of its highly polished wings bent and twisted out of shape.

Bringing down a buzz bomb with gunfire also presented its problems. Usually, the bombs were too fast to be overtaken in a normal dogfight pursuit unless the fighter made a diving attack. The most frequent method of attack was the deflection shot – approaching from the side and opening fire when the bomb crossed the pilot's line of sight.

Even though the pilotless planes flew straight and level, they presented difficulties that the Diver pilots had not run into before. The main trouble was with that sheet-steel skin. It not only mangled wing tips, but also deflected machine gun bullets like armour plate.

Cannon fire was the best weapon; a shell from a 20 mm cannon would blow a hole right through the steel outer covering. But a 20 mm cannon had a much shorter range than a .303 machine gun, forcing the attacking pilot to move in at close range before pressing the firing button. And if a cannon shell hit the Flying Bomb's 2,000 lb warhead, the result could be disastrous.

'Toasted' Spitfires and Tempests were not as common as bent wings from tipping but were frequent enough. When a buzz bomb blew up in mid-air, great chunks of metal shot about in all directions; some pieces were several feet long and weighed ten pounds or more. When this flying junk hit another aeroplane, the results were not very gratifying.

Jagged shrapnel holes and blasted-away control surfaces were the reward of careless or over-eager Diver pilots. Not that every pilot made it home to reflect upon his mistakes. At least five aircraft were destroyed by mid-air Flying Bomb explosions. One such aircraft, a Spitfire, was flown by a captain named Jean-Marie Maridor, who attacked a buzz bomb at point-blank range near the south coast. The bomb's ton of Trialen exploded in his face, blasting the Spitfire apart and killing Maridor instantly.

The aviators of Air Defence Great Britain were learning the lessons of the Flying Bomb in the air; at the same time, their superiors were learning them on the ground. During the first half of July, the nerve centre for the defence against the Flying Bomb was

'Some could even pull right alongside ...' The pilot of an RAF Spitfire moves into position next to a Flying Bomb ... and then begins lifting the left wing, 'tipping' the pilotless plane off course, 'flipping the Flying Bomb over and out of control'.

moved from Stanmore, Middlesex to Biggin Hill, just south-east of London. Stanmore was off in the countryside to the north and west of the capital, remote from the battle, while Biggin Hill was right in 'Buzz Bomb Alley'. During the Battle of Britain and the Blitz, Biggin Hill's location made it one of the RAF's most strategic airfields. Now, the base was back in the middle of a different kind of air action, this time as Diver Control.

Along with this move, the number of fighters assigned to Flying Bomb patrols was increased. Duncan Sandys ordered the defences to be increased to sixteen squadrons during the first week of July.

The actual combat experience of the flak gunners and fighter pilots, along with all the changes and countermeasures, were having their effect. Between 6th and 13th July, 57% of the Flying Bombs picked up by the Channel radar stations were destroyed by the defences – fighters, barrage balloons, and anti-aircraft – and only 34% were hitting London. But an average of 45 to 50 bombs were still getting through every day and causing, to use the official phrase, 'widespread damage'.

The best way of defeating the Flying Bombs was to destroy them before they were launched. Bomber Command and the US Army Air Force had dropped thousands of tons of bombs on suspected launching sites, but had not accomplished much so far.

In June, however, the French underground discovered a vast storehouse of the Flying Bombs within an hour's rail journey from the Pas de Calais. Hundreds of the bombs were stockpiled in the limestone caves of Saint-Leu-d'Esserent, north of Paris, hidden under several feet of shale and clay. This information was passed on to London at once. At last, after weeks of battling with the phantom-like launching ramps, the Allies had a target, an actual, real target, that could be pinned down and located on a map.

Normally, a heavy saturation-bombing raid would be called down on such a critical objective. But this was no ordinary target. Because the Flying Bombs were stowed away in caves, it would take several well-placed direct hits to destroy the site; near misses would only scatter a few rocks on top of the underground depot. A conventional air raid would be too imprecise for the task.

There was only one unit capable of doing the job without first going through a drawn-out training programme. Number 617

Squadron, RAF, was Bomber Command's élite unit, famous as the 'Dam Buster' squadron. The veterans of this outfit had carried out similar pin-point attacks in the past. Since mid-June, they had been armed with the 12,000 lb 'Tallboy' bomb, which they had dropped with deadly accuracy on targets in northern France. They would be able to bomb the caves with a minimum of time lost on preparation.

On this strike, 617 Squadron's four-engined Lancasters would once again be using the 6-ton 'Tallboy' bomb. The squadron commander would go in first, dropping smoke bombs from his American-built Mustang fighter; the rest of the group, seventeen Lancasters, would aim at the smoke.

On 4th July, the heavy clouds over northern France finally lifted, after a week-long wait, and 617 Squadron took off for the caves at Saint-Leu-d'Esserent. Each of the huge bombs found their mark. Seventeen times, the long, finned missiles buried themselves in the ground with a cloud of dust. A few seconds later the delayed action fuses detonated the six tons of explosives, making the earth erupt in a mushroom as high as a good sized office building.

Three days later, 617 Squadron attacked the caves again, putting the Saint-Leu-d'Esserent depot out of action. Twenty-five feet of chalk and clay avalanched into the caves, covering everyone and everything inside; the sealed entrances prevented any salvaging operations. Several hundred Flying Bombs were lost to Colonel Max Wachtel's *Flakregiment*.

In London, the results of this spectacular air raid were felt at once. Between 12.24 p.m. on 5th July and 8.32 a.m. on the 6th, a total of 60 Flying Bombs exploded within the Greater London area; the next day, only 14 bombs came down on the capital. The National Fire Service officially noted that 'A comparative freedom from attack was noticeable during the 24 hour period ...'

Over in the Pas de Calais, Unteroffizier Otto Neuchel could see rows and rows of wooden dollies, used for wheeling the Flying Bombs up to the launching ramps, standing empty in the soft summer drizzle. All day long, *Flakregiment* officers walked around with hands on hips and angry expressions. Sometimes a brass hat from Headquarters would drop by, and all the officers would get 'good and excited'.

Nobody told Neuchel anything, but nobody had to. The long

lines of empty dollies said more eloquently than any words that delivery of the Flying Bombs had stopped completely. It didn't take a genius to figure out why. Every day swarms of British and American planes flew overhead, on their way to bomb German installations farther inland.

During the next week the attack continued to be light – Otto Neuchel's unit fired only one bomb in three days – while the number of pilotless machines in the Pas de Calais remained scarce. But trainloads of the bombs soon began arriving from Central Germany, and the activities of *Flakregiment* 155(W) started to pick up again. On 13th July, less than a week after the second Saint-Leu-d'Esserent air strike, 42 of the machines exploded inside London's boundaries. The buzz bombs were back in force.

To US Intelligence worker Richard Baker, London looked emptier every day. Since Winston Churchill's speech on 6th July, thousands of women and children had already left London for safer areas to the north and west – beyond the range of the buzz bombs – and the evacuation was still in full swing.

An American reporter in *Newsweek* gave this impression of London during the V-1 Flying Bomb attack: Even during daylight hours the streets seem less crowded; after blackout, they were as deserted as during the Blitz. Sales of household goods and clothing were down by 30%, while travel items were up by 40%. In the suburbs, especially south of the Thames, wooden boards made ragged patches over blasted-out windows, while roped-off streets kept the curious – and looters – away from bomb-shattered buildings.

Most noticeable was the scarcity of children. Yeoman First Class Don Cumming doesn't recall ever having seen a child out playing, only out walking with a parent. Suburban streets took on an almost eerie quiet after the evacuation. By mid-July, Londoners were leaving at a rate of 15,000 a day, with trains crowded to standing capacity.

The evacuation was not the only sign of frayed nerves. Londoners, fed up with diving under tables and sleeping in damp basements, wanted a target for their frustration; the nearest and largest target was the government.

Three quarters of all the houses in Croydon, Surrey, just south of London, were damaged by Flying Bombs. The photo shows the Longmoor family standing by the wreckage of their home in Croydon, after a buzz bomb crashed on their street. When the bomb cut out, the three people ducked under a staircase and were saved from the falling bricks and beams.

The RAF hits back: 'On this strike 617 Squadron's four-engined Lancasters would once again be using the 6-ton ''Tallboy'' bomb. The 12,000 lb ''Tallboy'' bomb, which was used with great effect against the Flying Bomb storage caves at Saint-Leu-d'Esserent, with a Lancaster bomber in the background. Compare the height of the crewman with the size of the bomb.

Richard Baker was amazed to hear people blaming Winston Churchill for the bombs. Following a speech in the House of Commons, Baker heard several Londoners damning the Prime Minister out loud, a feeling that Baker could not understand. And the 15th July issue of the magazine *Picture Post* featured a three page photo-essay on the pilotless planes that began, 'Somebody in the British Government was caught napping by the Flying Bomb.'

Even though nerves were frayed and worn, people were determined not to let it show. It seemed like everyone who did not evacuate was as afraid of appearing afraid as of the bombs themselves. One resident of London pointed out that the behaviour of some of her neighbours, especially in a crowd, was 'unconcerned to the point of idiocy'. A buzz bomb would trundle over a queue of housewives outside a fishmonger's shop, tearing along full blast at rooftop height, and some of the women wouldn't even look up.

Margaret A. Hutcheson, an American Red Cross Staff aide, arrived in London during July 1944. She and the other Red Cross girls were 'fresh from the States', where they 'had only known friendly things in the skies'. On her first day in London, Miss Hutcheson was walking along a busy West End street when the air raid sirens went. Neither of them had any idea what the sound was, so they stopped a passer-by.

'Is that the noon whistle?' Miss Hutcheson asked, innocently. The man patiently answered, 'No, it's an air raid warning.'

During the trip over from America on the liner *Mauretania*, all the Red Cross girls were given a booklet on what to do in case of an air raid alert: they were to lie down, flat in the street, face toward the kerb. But no one was doing anything as dramatic as that. In fact, no one was doing anything at all. Miss Hutcheson didn't know what to do, so, once again, she asked the polite passer-by.

'We pay no attention?' she inquired.

'That's right,' the man replied.

The two smiled at each other and continued on their way, along with everyone else on the street.

Not every Flying Bomb roared harmlessly overhead. The buzz bombs were rolling up an impressive toll of killed and wounded, and continued to reduce war production in London by 25%. Not everyone killed by a pilotless plane was a Londoner, either. Early in

'... tearing along full-blast at roof-top height ...' A doodlebug scuttles towards London at low altitude.

July, a bomb came down on a US Army formation in Cadogan Square, Kensington. Scores of American soldiers were killed outright or badly injured.

One remedy for strung-out war nerves was to try and talk them away. Since the Number One Topic in London was the doodlebugs, people naturally chatted, day and night, about the things; nobody could do anything about them, so they might as well talk about them. Strange tales involving the sinister weapons were as common as the usual 'bomb stories', and were usually much more intriguing. A woman in Southwark was told, in all seriousness, that the buzz bombs were flown by the ghosts of dead Luftwaffe pilots.

Joking about the pilotless planes was another attempted cure for the jitters. In spite of everything, people still made up funny stories about the buzz bombs. In a well-known cartoon, a visibly upset man loudly scolds his cat, 'Purr if you must, but please don't *cut out* so suddenly!'

A West End textile firm distributed this form-letter to all of its employees one morning:

To facilitate the exchange of Flying Bomb experiences each morning, the following form should be completed and circulated throughout the Department together with the copy-letter.

My residence is situated in _____district, where the Alert lasted_____hours.

This period was spent in ...	house
	prayer
	shelter
My demeanour was ...	cool
	flustered
	absent
My child(ren) was/were ...	cheerful
	doleful
	frightful
	in the north of Scotland
My wife was ...	cool
	excited
	confined
	a damn nuisance

My house collapsed and
 the following were saved ...   me
                                   wife
                                   child(ren)
                                   dog
                                   canary
                                   tortoise
The following were casualties ... mother-in-law

I certify that I saw and heard more doodlebugs and was more seriously attacked and suffered generally to a greater extent than any other raidee.

....
(Signed)

Although London did its best to hide its anxiety, the stress and tension from the long Alerts still revealed itself. Public shelters were not as crowded as they were a few weeks before, mainly because many of the shelterers had left London, but they were full enough. People could put up with the buzz bombs in the daytime, but had to get away from them at night. Eight deep shelters, four on the north bank of the Thames and four on the south, were opened on 6th July. Each of these shelters, 100 feet underground, contained 8,000 bunks as well as a canteen and hospital facilities.

These new shelters were never as crowded as the stations of the London Underground. On most nights, the deep West End train stations were crammed. Some people actually lived 'down the tube', because they felt comfortable down in their own little club-like communities or, sometimes, because their homes had been blasted and they had nowhere else to go.

'The ones that were lucky enough to get a bunk were able to lie down,' recalls Miss Florence Cherry, a London Transport employee who worked at Holloway Road Underground Station in North London. 'But the others couldn't spread out until the last trains had gone through,' when they spread out all over the platform.

The same 'deep shelter mentality' as 1940 had returned, and along with it came the same discomforts – stale, putrid air; over-flowing latrines; lice; 'shelter cough'; and dirty, unchanged clothing. Although the station staff did their best to keep the Underground shelters clean, hygiene was almost non-existent.

At Holloway Road Station, shelterers would tramp down the steps with their bundles of bedding in the late afternoon and, next morning, carried them back up again. Some dropped their bundles off at the coffee shop next door, where they were minded for two shillings (10 pence) per week. 'They were never even aired,' Florence Cherry pointed out, 'so you can imagine the smell.' Frequently some of the shelterers would urinate in the fire buckets during the night, or else 'mess in paper and leave it in the waste frames' on the platform.

Hilda Neal of South Kensington, who had talked herself out of going to shelter a few weeks earlier, finally gave in on 6th July. 'I slept on a top bunk in the Albert Hall shelter tunnel,' she later reported, 'in a small room with about seven people. It was rather weird, but not at all comfortable. The shelter was crammed ...' even though many of her neighbours preferred to shelter at home. Some local people she spoke with informed her that 'the basements of all the houses were full to overflowing'.

Spending the night in the tunnel shelter was not exactly luxurious. 'Never in my wildest dreams would I have thought I'd ever sleep under such conditions ...' stuffy, noisy from the loud blowers, a light burning all night. 'Left at 7 a.m. feeling like nothing on earth.' Before she left, the woman in the bunk under hers said that only two of the eighty-five houses on her street were habitable; the rest were bomb-blasted shells.

Although the Underground platforms and public shelters were usually at their capacity, actually only a small percentage of the population slept in these. A few brave souls shunned any type of shelter. Dennis Horsford of St John's Wood mentions that, 'My wife and I had long since ceased to lose sleep by sheltering in the basement – we took out chances on the sixth floor of a ten-floor building.'

But this sort of tranquillity was rare. Most people had some sort of shelter at home and used it regularly. Some simply went down into the basement at night; others moved into their back garden Anderson shelter. A third kind of home shelter used indoors was the Morrison Shelter, which US Navy Yeoman Don Cumming described as 'a massive steel table strong enough to withstand the impact of falling debris'.

Don Cumming had struck up an acquaintance with an English family, the Kents, who lived in Purley, Surrey, and spent an occasional week-end at their home. Purley is situated about eleven miles south of Central London, right in 'Buzz Bomb Alley', and the Kent family was prepared for the worst. They had a Morrison shelter installed in one of the bedrooms.

Three of the shelter's four sides were covered with a heavy wire mesh. On the inside, 'under the table', Mrs Kent hung a bag full of wet cloths for breathing through – in case the house was badly damaged, flying plaster dust would not choke everybody. There was also a whistle to guide diggers to the spot. Wallets and shoes were also kept inside the shelter, and everyone dressed warmly enough to be able to endure a long wait for rescuers.

A Morrison was only wide enough to sleep three people full length; when Cumming came to call, everybody – Mr Kent, Mrs Kent, their daughter Jean, and Don Cumming – slept with their legs sticking out one side of the shelter. Whenever a Doodlebug was heard in the distance, someone would shout, 'Pull up your feet!'

Purley was the home of roughly 20,000 to 30,000 residents, but Don Cumming thinks that there were no more than a hundred houses that still had all their walls and windows intact. The Kents were among the fortunate. Their house suffered only a few panes of glass out of the front door, some plaster fallen into the sitting room, and a door or two knocked out of plumb.

On 21st July a buzz bomb crashed into Barchester Street, a residential avenue in Bow, East London, one of the 41 incidents that occurred that day. Thirty houses were destroyed and a large two-storey building was severely damaged by fire and explosion; seven were killed, and nineteen seriously injured. Sixty-three Flying Bombs hit London the next day. One of these killed and injured 175 people in West London. Each Trialen bomb had the blast equivalent of the two ton 'blockbuster' bombs dropped on Berlin by the RAF.

D-Day had been six weeks before. Although news headlines made every effort to sound optimistic – especially after an assassination attempt barely missed killing Hitler on 20th July – a good many people were having their doubts. Over in France, the war still ground slowly along. Even after the Norman city of Caen fell on 9th July, hailed as a 'key objective', the hoped-for breakout from the Normandy beachhead did not happen. And the Flying Bombs kept on coming.

CHAPTER FIVE

'The Doodlebugs Are Finished ... We Hope!'

The two planes went into a wide circle, low and fast, as though they were looking for something. Unteroffizier Otto Neuchel couldn't tell if they were British or American, but knew that they weren't 'ours' without even looking. He had not seen a Luftwaffe aeroplane since his unit arrived in the Pas de Calais.

It was anything but reassuring, watching those low-winged 'Spitfires' – to Neuchel, any enemy fighter, British or American, was a Spitfire. He knew that they attacked anything that moved, even a man on a bicycle.

The air raid alarm had been given and everybody had taken cover; Neuchel was watching the planes from a slit trench. But that would not help much if a cannon shell or a bomb touched off the warhead of the Flying Bomb that stood only a few yards from Neuchel's catapult. The bomb was right out in plain sight, where Neuchel and his crew left it when the alarm sounded. If that went off it would take everything, and probably everyone, along with it.

Eventually, the two planes wheeled off to the south-west, apparently without spotting anything. But they, or other 'Spitfires', would be back later. Enemy planes were always snooping about; sometimes flights of eight or more would come close enough so that Neuchel could see the colour of their propeller spinners. None of them had seen anything yet, but there was always a first time.

Unteroffizier Neuchel had more confidence in the attacks than any British or American air commander. In the month of July 1944 the RAF and US Army Air Force flew more than 1,000 sorties against Flying Bomb targets in France; the results were negligible. Except for the 'Tallboy' attacks on the Saint-Leu-d'Esserent caves, no real let-up in the Flying Bomb attack was noticed. Strafing attacks against the launching ramps were the most frustrating – whole new sites could be re-assembled within hours. The official verdict was that the attempt to stop the Flying Bomb on the ground was a failure.

But Hitler's bid to draw the Allied bombers away from Germany's cities had also failed. Although 20% of US and British air strength was being aimed at Flying Bomb objectives, the Reich itself was still being pounded steadily.

On 7th July, 2,000 Allied bombers struck at a wide array of targets within Germany. During the month of July the US 8th Air Force alone dropped 45,000 tons of high explosives – this does not include the RAF or any other US Army Air Force units. While the Luftwaffe kept firing its pilotless aircraft across the Channel, Allied bombers continued to toggle their payloads over the Ruhr and Rhine valley.

Since the Flying Bombs could not be destroyed before launching, the only other option was to shoot them out of the air. Fighters and anti-aircraft were bringing down several hundred each week, but too many of the machines were still getting through.

Something would have to be done, and quickly, to tighten the defensive screen. One suggestion was to move all the flak guns from the North Downs to the Channel Coast. This would put the batteries forty miles closer to the approaching buzz bombs. It would also give the gunners a clear field of fire, and allow them to arm their shells with American proximity fuses – these new fuses were expected to be deadly against the straight-and-level flying pilotless planes.

Each electronic proximity fuse was fitted with a small radio transmitter and a receiver unit. After the anti-aircraft shell was fired, the fuse's transmitter began sending out a signal; the signal bounced off the target and was picked up by the receiver. When the shell came close to its target the bouncing echo detonated the fuse, spraying the area with a lethal hail of steel splinters.

Proximity fuses were much more accurate than the conventional type of fuse, especially at low altitudes, but the close mid-air bursts could also endanger civilian lives and property. Over the Channel, however, the shock waves and jagged chunks of metal would only rough up the water's already choppy surface.

In the middle of July 1944, every anti-aircraft crew in the North Downs got some unexpected orders: prepare to move out for the south coast. On 13th July, four hundred twelve 3.7-inch guns began their journey southward. Along with the guns went 2,300 men and women, 60,000 tons of supplies and ammunition, and 3,000 miles of cable.

The journey was made in the remarkable time of only four days – everything was in position by 17th July. One gunner, remembering the transfer, described it as 'four solid days of grunting, sweating, and cursing'.

By 19th July an additional 572 20 mm and 40 mm guns of the Royal Artillery and US Army, along with 584 light guns from the RAF, had arrived. More than 2,500 guns and 700 rocket tubes made up this new Gun Belt, which stretched for roughly sixty miles along the Channel coast.

In front of the guns, out over the Channel, and also behind the anti-aircraft screen flew the Spitfires and Tempests of the Diver Patrols. The fighters above the Channel intercepted any incoming buzz bombs before the machines could reach the coast; the inland patrols would pick up any bombs that got past the guns. Behind the fighters and flak batteries waited the steel cables of the barrage balloons.

An RAF officer called this new defensive set up 'a hard comb with many teeth'. Duncan Sandys, General Pile, and the RAF chiefs hoped the remodelled defences would live up to their increased expectations.

But General Erich Heinemann and the Luftwaffe High Command also had a few changes. At the end of July Colonel Max Wachtel and his *Flakregiment* were ordered to begin salvoing the Flying Bombs, launching thirty or more at the same time. The Luftwaffe commanders were hoping to swamp the British defences, putting so many pilotless planes in the air that the fighter pilots and gunners would not be able to handle them all.

None of the men in the Flying Bomb launch crews were wildly enthusiastic about the new order. This 'timing' business was just one more thing to worry about. To Unteroffizier Otto Neuchel, it was also another excuse for catapult officers to shout and bully. He and his crew used to push the bombs up to the catapult at their own pace, but now there was always someone watching them, scolding them, ordering them to move faster.

One officer in particular went out of his way to be a damn nuisance. Unteroffizier Neuchel and his crew had christened this big-mouthed junior officer 'General Shithead'. One of General Shithead's more endearing habits was to stand behind Neuchel and shout, 'Firing Time is in twenty minutes! Hurry up! Move!' along with other words of encouragement.

And after the bomb was ready on the ramp, everybody would usually have to stand about and wait anyway, mostly because some unit up the line had broken down. Sometimes, the waiting would last an hour or more.

Watching the ramps fire all at once was quite a sight, though, especially at night. Sometimes thirty catapults would launch simultaneously. All round, the noise of the pulse jets created a continuous din. Then the catapults were fired and the little fire-tailed aeroplanes shot off toward the north, like candles in a procession, and disappeared.

Crashes were still routine. Now, with simultaneous launchings, there were also simultaneous crashes. Otto Neuchel remembers one night when five Flying Bombs crashed at the same time, just after take-off. 'The entire world turned red' from the explosions, and the noise was terrible. Neuchel found out later on that three ramps had been destroyed and about a dozen men killed by the concussion.

The idea of overwhelming the defences worked better than anyone expected. Flying Bombs began slipping through in bunches, crashing in scattered areas of London within minutes of each other. Seven buzz bombs came to earth within 12 minutes, between 3.23 and 3.35 p.m., on 27th July. Just over two hours later, in the quarter of an hour between 5.45 and 6.00, seventeen of the bombs hit and exploded. On the 29th, eleven came down during a ten minute stretch in mid-afternoon.

For two weeks, the Flying Bombs kept on landing in clusters – sometimes three or four would land within seconds of each other. The anti-aircraft and fighter screen, still not fully co-ordinated after the move to the coast, bagged their fair share, but the bombs kept swarming through.

The climax came on 3rd August, when 101 Flying Bombs crash-

A HARD COMB WITH MANY TEETH — Barrage balloons, the anti-aircraft gun belt, and 'Diver' patrols combined to bring down hundreds of Flying Bombs before they could reach London. Home Chain and Home Chain (Low) radar stations kept track of the pilotless planes on their journey across the Channel.

dived into Greater London's one hundred square-mile radius. During the early morning hours an average of one bomb every six minutes struck, lighting up the sky with the same brilliant red flashes that had alarmed Otto Neuchel while inside his slit trench in the Pas de Calais. So efficient was the Flying Bomb's fusing system that only four out of 2,700 incidents were classified 'unexploded' during the pilotless attack.

If the news about the Flying Bombs wasn't bad enough, Military Intelligence now had something else to worry about. New pieces of evidence convinced the experts in Winston Churchill's War Cabinet that the A-4 long-range rocket would very soon be ready for operations against Britain.

On 13th June, an A-4 fired from Peenemünde went astray and came down in southern Sweden. After some tricky negotiating between the British and neutral Swedish governments, British Intelligence was able to acquire the rocket fragments. The scientific branch of Military Intelligence began rebuilding the missile.

From their reconstruction, the scientists learned that the rocket had only a one-ton warhead – estimates of up to 10 tons had been predicted – but also found that the A-4 had the range and performance for hitting targets in southern England. Other evidence (aerial photos, reports from the Polish underground) indicated that the enemy had manufactured at least 1,000 A-4s by June. Word of the regular tests at Blinza, also sent by the Polish underground, seemed to be decisive proof of the A-4's readiness.

Actually, the tests on the A-4 at Blinza were still giving General Dornberger and Wernher von Braun as much trouble as ever. That mid-air burst just would not be solved. Eighty-five per cent of the test-fired rockets were still exploding high up in the earth's atmosphere. Every effort was being made to work out this stubborn defect, but in July 1944, the A4 was nowhere near being ready for operations against British targets.

London, however, had convinced itself otherwise. The fragments of the crashed Swedish rocket persuaded everyone, even those who had ridiculed the very thought of a long-range rocket not so long ago, of the weapon's feasibility. At the end of July Duncan Sandys thought that a rocket attack might come at any time.

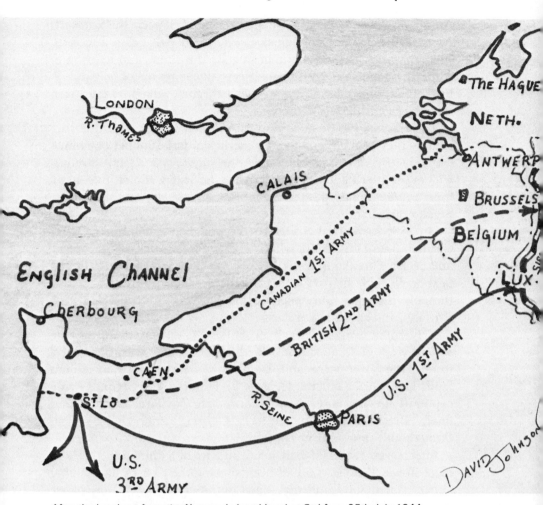

After the breakout from the Normandy beachhead at St Lô on 25th July 1944, the Allied armies ran across France. By the first week of September all Flying Bomb launch sites had been captured, and the British, American, and Canadian divisions faced the Siegfried Line defences.

An air of weary resignation had taken hold of even the hardiest. Richard Baker of US Intelligence, who steadfastly refused to go to shelter, was awakened one morning by the sirens and a string of stuttering doodlebugs. Still half asleep, Baker got out of bed, put on his helmet, and took refuge in the bathroom, which he had been told was safer than the bedroom.

There seemed to be no end to the pilotless machines. All during the day they kept chug-chugging overhead, dark silhouettes against the grey overcast, and disturbed the night with their powerful, window-shattering blast. But during the last week of July news from France finally gave everyone something else to think about besides buzz bombs.

On 25th July, the US First Army punched a hole through the German lines at St Lô, in what General Eisenhower called 'a clear and decisive breakout' from the Normandy beachhead. During the next week, US, British, and Canadian troops continued to rush through the gap and began branching out to the west, into Brittany, and east, toward Paris.

A German counter-attack at Falaise was routed during the second week of August, and Allied forces kept on with their drive toward the River Seine and, beyond the Seine, the Flying Bomb launching sites. General George S. Patton's US Second Army captured the Brittany U-Boat ports of St Nazaire, Lorient, and finally Brest on 19th August. The German armies fell back all throughout France during the month of August.

After seven weeks of bad news and wishful thinking, this was more like it. People who had been shaking their heads and talking about stalemate suddenly had nothing to say. Newspaper headlines, which had struggled to sound optimistic during the past few weeks, now outdid themselves in describing the drive across France. In its 2nd August edition, the *News Chronicle* announced, 'ALLIES ENGULF WHOLE GERMAN FRONT IN NORMANDY.'

London ate up the headlines. The news from across the Channel crowded the buzz bombs not only from the front pages of newspapers, but also out of most conversations. Neighbours who had spoken in tight voices about 'those things' began greeting each other with, 'Have you heard the latest from over there?' Even complaints about the weather began to creep in.

Not that the Flying Bombs had stopped. General Bradley's and Field Marshal Montgomery's armies were still a long way from the Pas de Calais launching ramps. A typical entry in a summer 1944 diary complains: 'Doodlebugs all yesterday. Alerts every few minutes.'

'Looking out to the south just now we see ... glittering in the sunset, the thick line of barrage balloons stretching from Sydenham to Croydon,' Mrs Gwladys Cox noted in her flat in West Hampstead. The Flying Bomb defences had become as much a part of the scenery as the sunset.

Fear of the buzz bombs darkened the good news from Normandy and kept Londoners bunked down in their air raid shelters. Spending a night in bed instead of the shelter was a momentous occasion, worth a phone call to a friend the next day, or a note in the diary.

Some aspects of buzz bomb watching were not always unpleasant, though. A woman in the Notting Hill district of London invited a few neighbours over for a get-together; they sat on the steps to keep away from the windows. As they chatted away on their somewhat uncomfortable perches, half-listening for the sound of a pulse-jet in the distance, everyone was aware of how close they all felt toward each other – a feeling that would never return in peace-time.

Owners of very elegant and expensive restaurants found little comfort in the Flying Bomb threat. Many had to close down their businesses – nobody would come into a cafe where they might be cut by blast-propelled slivers of crystal or mirror-glass. Managers of hotels and blocks of flats were having a hard time letting rooms on the south side of their building – the side that faced the approaching doodlebugs.

The Flying Bombs did not stop American pilot Truman Smith from coming back to London on leave. He finally did get to see a buzz bomb, and had heard quite a few hair-raising tales about the bombs. But his unit's base, Great Ashfield, Suffolk, had also been hit by a stray Flying Bomb – Great Ashfield is about 65 miles north-east of London – so he decided that there was nowhere to escape to.

On this trip, Truman Smith and a fighter pilot he met on the train down to London checked into the Savoy Hotel, for a 'real change in barracks life'. They followed the bellboy up to their room, when Smith asked, 'Which way do they come from?'

The bellboy knew what he meant and replied, 'Oh, you can see 'em comin', sir.'

'Hell, I don't *want* to see 'em comin'! We want a room on the other side of the hotel!' Smith insisted.

There were no vacancies on the 'other side' of the hotel, the bellboy informed them. Which explained why they had no trouble getting a room at the Savoy. Only 'dumb Yank combat pilots' would sleep on the side overlooking the Thames, facing Buzz Bomb Alley.

On their first night, the two flyers found out why nobody wanted to stay in the Savoy's south-facing rooms. Truman Smith and his fighter pilot room-mate retired at about midnight, after an evening at the theatre. A Flying Bomb would chug over from time to time, keeping the fighter jockey awake. Smith, however, had no trouble at all sleeping – 'I can sleep better than I can fly. One of my better talents,' he admitted.

A short while later, he was jolted awake by a roaring explosion. Smith hadn't heard the buzz bomb coming, and opened his eyes in time to see the elegant window drapes stretched out horizontally by the blast – neither of them had noticed that the glass in their large fourth-storey window was missing, blown out by an earlier bomb.

That was enough for the 'Jug' pilot. He poured himself a large drink, announced to Smith, 'I'm checkin' out right now and going back to base,' and left without further ceremony. Smith went back to sleep, intending to stay another night at the Savoy. His leave would not expire for another 24 hours; he had no plans for returning before then.

On 7th August, the 2,000th Flying Bomb hit London. The defences were now destroying a much larger percentage of the machines than a few weeks before, but about 25 per day still exploded within the capital. The main thing that kept London's spirits up was the belief that the Allied armies would soon push the Flying Bomb launch crews right out of the Pas de Calais and out of range of London.

News from France kept getting better all the time. The

'The thick line of barrage balloons ...' stretch as far as the eye can see, protecting the southern approaches to London.

American, British, and Canadian advance was, in General Eisenhower's words, 'weeks ahead of schedule'. Motorised columns, under air cover, swept ahead in advances of ten, fifteen, and sometimes twenty miles a day.

On 15th August, ten American and French divisions landed on southern France's Mediterranean coast, and began moving north to link up with the D-Day troops. Four days later, the banner headline of the *News Chronicle* proclaimed: GERMANS ROUTED IN FRANCE, NORMANDY BATTLE IS WON.

A special broadcast on 23rd August brought the best news yet – Paris had been liberated. The announcement caused no wild celebrations in London's streets, but everyone realised that a key objective had been taken from the enemy. On the day after Paris was freed, Westminster Abbey and St Paul's Cathedral rang their bells in celebration for the first time in weeks – it was feared that their peals might drown out the sound of an approaching buzz bomb.

On the same day, Otto Neuchel's firing unit launched their last Flying Bomb at London. Later in the day, Neuchel's unit and several others were ordered out of the Calais area. Nobody knew where they were going – some rumours said Holland; others mentioned Germany.

All day long and well into the night, Unteroffizier Neuchel and his crew kept on loading stores and equipment aboard trucks. Nobody had any sleep, there were only cold field rations to eat, and their old friend General Shithead was always around to make life miserable.

Still, Neuchel reasoned, it was better than being blown up by a crashed Flying Bomb. And, with any luck, General Shithead might burst a blood vessel.

As Unteroffizier Neuchel eventually found out by word-of-mouth, Colonel Max Wachtel's *Flakregiment* 155(W) was ordered to withdraw to a camp outside Antwerp, in Belgium. From there, they would take up a position for firing against Continental targets.

While the firing units were slowly falling back, elements of the German 15th Army remained in the Pas de Calais area to slow down the Allied drive. Their resistance gave the Luftwaffe crews time to take all their equipment along with them, while some units remained in place and continued to fire at London.

On 24th August, the same day that Otto Neuchel got his orders to move, Mrs Gwladys Cox's flat in Cholmley Gardens, West Hampstead suffered a very near miss. An Alert made Mrs Cox and her husband Ralph glance out from their balcony. They were greeted by the sight of a buzz bomb headed directly for their building.

'Suddenly it stopped, dipped, and slowly and steadily dived nose-down. We were so spellbound ... that we actually watched it for a few seconds.' They snapped out of it though, and 'dashed back into our hall for shelter,' just in time. 'Immediately, there was a violent explosion and a shattering of windows on all sides.'

Fortunately for the Coxes, their windows were the only casualties. A little farther up the road, the residents did not get off so lightly. The Flying Bomb destroyed several buildings, and also killed and injured a number of people. Later on, Mrs Cox went out to look at the wreckage. She found that 'Some twenty houses have been blasted to mere shells; front doors, furniture, personal belongings blown out into the gardens.'

Two days later, however, on 26th August, London received its first Flying Bomb-free day in eleven weeks. No sirens sounded, day or night. The official report summarises: 'This is the longest lull enjoyed by London since the Flying Bomb attacks began in earnest.'

The lull was largely due to the slowdown in firing by Colonel Wachtel's retreating *Flakregiment*. But the defences were also responsible, especially the flak guns. The gun belt was now destroying most of the pilotless machines before they reached the coast.

After the guns were moved from the North Downs to the Channel coast, their scores began improving at once. Also, new equipment finally began to arrive at the beginning of August – American made SCR-584 radar sets, and the long-awaited proximity fuses. It took a while before everybody got used to the new gear, but, after the novelty wore off, the results were dramatic and immediate.

The proximity fuses quickly began proving their worth. From their first day, the radio-activated fuses destroyed any number of Flying Bombs that would have got through against conventionally-fused shells.

Just as effective were the SCR-584 radar sets. Linked to the gun's power system, the new radar turned and elevated the flak batteries automatically; the anti-aircraft crew simply loaded the gun. Everything else was done by the radar set, which locked on to its target and followed it along its course, keeping the gun barrel pointed at the Flying Bomb. Together in this strange new war, the two components all but did away with the human element – automatic guns tracked and shot at flights of pilotless planes.

Adding their own brand of detachment to the battle against the Flying Bombs were the barrage balloons. Over 200 of the bombs had been brought down by the balloons' steel mooring cables so far. Sometimes a low-flying buzz bomb would smack into a cable and explode dramatically in mid-air, littering the surrounding area with huge chunks of twisted metal.

Not every unit in the fight against the doodlebugs was fully mechanical, though. In North London, Albert Dudmesh worked the night shift at his job and was also a member of the local Home Guard. One of his Home Guard duties was to man a Lewis gun on top of a 12-foot high pillbox. Whenever the announcement 'Home Guard testing!' sounded over the public address system – the signal that a Flying Bomb was approaching – he would 'run like blazes' for his post, where he was supposed to begin shooting at the intruding doodlebug.

It was about a quarter-mile flat-out dash to the pillbox, then up a perpendicular iron ladder to the top, while the Flying Bomb was boring in at over 300 miles per hour. Every time Dudmesh reached his gun post the spotter would tell him, 'Sorry, mate, you're too late' – the buzz bomb was long gone by then. Sometimes the day shift would add to the frustration. From time to time, they would conscientiously remove the Lewis gun from its position, dismantle it and pack it inside the pillbox, leaving the out of breath Dudmesh not only without a target, but also without a gun.

Along the Channel coast, however, the number of Flying Bombs brought down increased with each passing week. Seventy four per cent were destroyed during the third week of August. London newspapers gave the battle full coverage; at the end of August, a party of ninety-five London Civil Defence members were taken to the south coast to watch the anti-aircraft batteries in action.

While the fascinated audience looked on, the 3.7-inchers opened

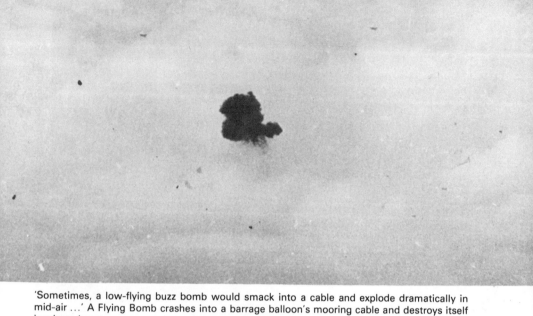

'Sometimes, a low-flying buzz bomb would smack into a cable and explode dramatically in mid-air ...' A Flying Bomb crashes into a barrage balloon's mooring cable and destroys itself in a huge burst.

'... littering the surrounding area with huge chunks of twisted metal.' The wreckage of a destroyed buzz bomb is gathered into a pile by the balloon's handling crew.

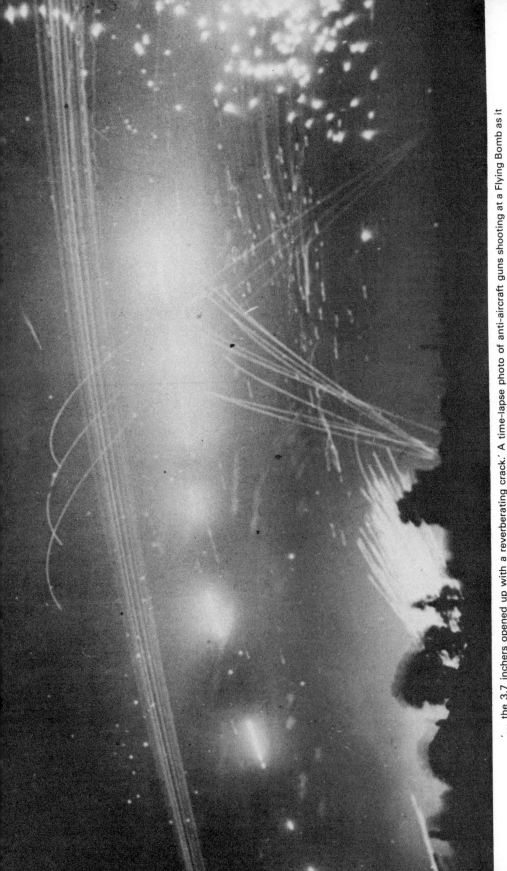

'... the 3.7 inchers opened up with a reverberating crack.' A time-lapse photo of anti-aircraft guns shooting at a Flying Bomb as it crashes to earth. The large flashes across the picture are from the bomb's pulsating jet engine.

up with their reverberating crack. Out over the Channel, black bursts of shellfire began popping all round a fast-moving silhouette, dark and low in the sky. A burst nicked the left wing; the bomb lurched to the left, steadied itself, and dived straight into the Channel with a muffled roar.

General Frederick Pile, the commanding general of Anti-Aircraft Command, encouraged the group to 'tell them all about it' after they went back home to London.

The news certainly did get around. 'A record bag of Flying Bombs today,' Mrs Gwladys Cox remarked on 28th August. 'Out of 101 ... 97 were brought down and only four reached London.'

Mrs Cox's figures were actually a bit off. Ninety-seven Flying Bombs had approached the coast; the guns shot down 65, the fighters 23, and the balloons got 2, for a grand total of 90. But the message was the same: the Flying Bomb had been defeated.

Only four or five bombs per day were now hitting London, a sharp drop from the early part of the month. The German armies, pursued by British, American, and Canadian spearheads, continued to flee eastward, abandoning the Flying Bomb launching ramps to the Allied forces. '14 More Sites Taken,' announced the *News Chronicle* on 30th August.

The rumours that Unteroffizier Otto Neuchel had heard about going to Holland turned out to be right after all. His unit was supposed to have set up camp just outside of Antwerp, but the advancing British armies chased them right out of the area. During the first few days of September, Neuchel and his unit arrived near 'some dreary little Dutch village', where they stopped to await further orders.

'RETREAT OF GERMANS BECOMES A ROUT' was the *Daily Telegraph*'s headline on 1st September. Every other London newspaper, and every news broadcast on the BBC, kept up a string of cheery announcements. 'More good news today,' was a frequent remark in letters and diaries during the early days of September 1944.

The France-based Flying Bomb attack ended on 1st September, when the last of the Pas de Calais catapults were captured. On 4th September Field Marshal Montgomery's armies entered the

Belgian port of Antwerp, giving the Allies another deep-water harbour. The US First Army was coming up to the very border of Germany and the Siegfried Line defences; farther south, General Patton's Third Army also moved steadily toward the Siegfried positions.

'The burning question of the day is: "How long will the war last?" ' wondered Mrs Gwladys Cox. To readers of *The Times* and the *Express*, it looked like the British, Canadian, and American armies would be inside Germany within a few weeks, if not days.

But the Allied armies were in no position to rush behind the Siegfried Line. German troops still occupied any number of strategic strongholds, including the seaward approaches to Antwerp, that would have to be dealt with first. Uprooting these pockets would be a time-consuming operation.

The largest problem facing the troops at the German border was not the enemy positions, however. It was supplies. Everything – all equipment, ammunition, food, and replacement troops – had to be brought up by trucks from the beachhead area, 450 miles across France.

No forward depots had been built during the headlong rush across France – there had been no time. The supply lines never caught up with the advance. Now, the armies would have to sit and wait while storage depots were established in eastern France. Any drives into Germany would have to be postponed until then.

There was little concern about the supply problem in British government circles, though. The Flying Bomb sites in France had been overrun, and the Allied timetable on the Continent was estimated to be running eight months ahead of schedule. On 1st September, 1944 all Air Raid Wardens' posts were ordered to discontinue lectures and training as a precaution against 'the rocket bomb (V-2)' – only five weeks after Duncan Sandys worried that a rocket attack might come any day.

Newspapers were even allowed to run small items on the mysterious 'V-2', never giving any details, however. Since the government believed that the rocket sites would also be overrun before the missiles could be launched against Britain, censorship rules were relaxed. Winston Churchill had already mentioned the guided missile in a speech before the House of Commons on 2nd

August, warning that 'long-range rockets' might be used against London in the very near future.

The *Daily Telegraph* ran a small item headed, 'V-2 Ready, Say Germans', on 14th August. The piece went on to say that the new weapon was not like the V-1 Flying Bomb, but was 'something absolutely new'. On 26th August the *News Chronicle* carried a story on the US Army Air Force attack on 'The Peenemünde Flying Bomb and rocket experimental station'.

Some of the reports were fairly frightening. The *News Chronicle* printed an article on 29th August that began: 'V-2: THREE REPORTS – V-2 was described yesterday as: 1, a myth; 2, an ice bomb; 3, a 40,000 lb rocket.' *The New Yorker* magazine thought the V-2 might be an incendiary fog sprayed from enemy planes, or maybe something to do with splitting the atom.

Major General Dornberger and Wernher von Braun guessed that over 65,000 changes had been made in the A-4 rocket. Everything from warhead weight to wiring and fuel lines had been modified. By the end of August, most of the major problems had been worked out of the rocket's system – including the stubborn 'air burst' problem.

It turned out that the fuel tanks had been causing all the difficulties. Heat and vibration from lifting off were jarring the tanks and making them crack, spraying the supply of alcohol and liquid oxygen inside the missile and causing an explosion. Once the problem was discovered, the solution was simple enough. Reinforced outer skins were riveted to the fuel tanks at the underground Central Works factory, strengthening the tanks and preventing further fractures. From then on the A-4 rocket was ready for operations against enemy targets, carrying a warhead as powerful as the Flying Bomb's.

After the rockets had finally passed all their tests, the launching troops were ordered into position to begin firing on London. By 7th September all units were in position: 444 (Training and Experimental) Battery's three mobile launching platforms and all its vehicles rolled up to the Dutch-German border, and 485 (Mobile) Artillery Detachment moved its nine launching units set up camp near The Hague, in Holland. The troops of 485

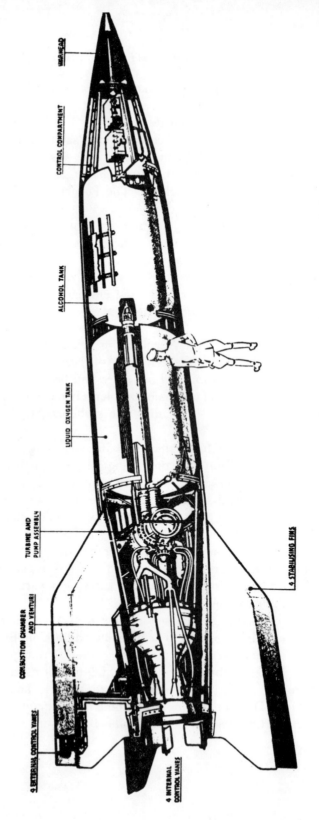

An A-4 (V-2) rocket, illustrating internal systems and controls (*National Archives*, USA).

Detachment, equipped with fully operational A-4 rockets, were just under 200 miles from London.

Nine Flying Bombs hit London on 1st September, the parting shots fired by *Flakregiment* 155(W)'s Pas de Calais ramps. The rest of the week was totally free of buzz bombs; the sirens didn't sound even once. A woman from Croydon made a quick note in her pocket diary, 'The doodlebugs are finished ... we hope!' Mrs Gwladys Cox was moved to report, 'No Flying Bombs. *What* a relief!' a sentiment shared by every other Londoner.

Mrs Cox wasn't the only one who was relieved. On 3rd September all British air commanders were ordered to suspend any further counter-offensives against the V-2 rockets; after 30th August, the US Army Air Force flew no more sorties against suspected launching sites.

Two days later the Vice Chiefs of Staff confirmed this move, announcing that all launching areas were as good as captured by the onrushing Allied armies.

A few RAF commanders did not agree. They pointed out that the rockets did have a range of over 200 miles; the sites within this 200-mile radius had not yet been captured; and recommended that every step be taken to knock out this new weapon before it could be used against them. But these warnings were ignored in the general feeling of relief. The Flying Bombs had been beaten and, everybody agreed, the V-2 rocket presented no possible danger.

On 7th September, Herbert Morrison, the Minister of Home Security, officially ordered an end to the evacuation of London. Later that same day, Duncan Sandys gave a statement to the press on the German secret weapons. Sandys came right to the point. In his first sentence, he told the reporters, 'Except for a last few shots, the Battle of London is over.'

CHAPTER SIX

'An Extraordinary Thunderclap'

Sixty-four year-old Robert Stubbs slowly made his way across the playing field of the Staveley Road School, in the West London suburb of Chiswick. As caretaker of the school, Stubbs put in a full day at his job. He still had a few chores left to do even though it was well past six o'clock in the evening.

Most residents of Staveley Road had already arrived home from work as the clock approached 7 p.m. on Friday, 8th September 1944. Because of the misty drizzle that had been falling all afternoon, and now threatened to turn into a steady rain, everybody stayed indoors behind their blackout curtains. Only one other person was out under the dark clouds. Stubbs caught sight of an army private walking briskly past the neat houses, on his way to visit his girl friend.

At 6.44 Stubbs was picked up and hurled twenty feet across the playing field by an overwhelming blast. There had been no warning at all: Stubbs was walking slowly along the school grounds; the next instant, he lay sprawled out on the grass.

After getting up on his feet, he was astonished to find the houses on both sides of the street demolished. Most had no roof. All that was left of some houses was a single free-standing wall rising above a pile of rubble.

Stubbs staggered over to the nearest wrecked dwelling, where he saw a grey haired woman crawling out of the ruins. He tried to do something to help, but by the time the ambulance and rescue squads arrived the 65-year-old woman had died.

Robert Stubbs had been lucky. The explosion killed two people outright, including Private Frank Browning, who had been walking to his girl friend's house. Twenty others had been injured, trapped inside their smashed homes. Eleven houses were totally destroyed; another 27 were seriously damaged and had to be evacuated.

People from nearby streets began filtering over to Staveley Road to see what had caused the sudden and very loud noise, which one witness described as sounding 'just like a gas main going off'. They found a crater, about 30 feet wide and 10 feet deep, in the middle of the road. Neighbouring houses had been blasted into piles of debris. Ambulance attendants methodically bandaged the wounds of those who had been pulled out of the wreckage by the Rescue Squad.

Two RAF officers soon arrived and began prowling about inside the crater. They picked up bits of metal and, after a quick inspection, dropped them into their briefcases. The two were eventually joined by American officers and London Civil Defence officials.

A reporter cornered one of the Civil Defence men and asked if the explosion could have been caused by some new kind of robot bomb. Any reply would have been strictly off the record – censors would allow no mention of the incident in the press, the reporter realised – but the CD official refused to give any information. 'We can't tell you what it was,' he said. 'It might have been a gas main explosion.' The reporter didn't believe the story; the Civil Defence man didn't expect him to.

Mrs Gwladys Cox also heard the explosion in her flat in West Hampstead. She was listening to the radio, sitting with her cat on her lap; the sudden jarring boom shook the chair and startled the cat, making the animal jump up to its feet.

A few seconds later, her husband Ralph came running in. 'Had you heard *that* one?' he shouted. Cox described the noise as 'a single, very loud crack ... something like that of a gun.'

'I just wonder if it is some munitions works explosion,' Mrs Cox thought to herself, '*or* the heralded V-2!'

All over London, people heard the loud report. Sixteen seconds after the Staveley Road explosion, another unexplained blast rocked the district of Epping, in north-west London, causing no casualties. Londoners could only guess at what it was. Some thought it was another Flying Bomb; others doubted that it was a buzz bomb because there had been no air raid Alert.

US Intelligence worker Richard Baker was told that a bomber had crashed. Hilda Neal of South Kensington thought it must have been 'an extraordinary thunderclap, as there was no reverberation'. After thinking about it for a while, Miss Neal added, 'Some new horror, I suppose.'

Duncan Sandys heard the explosion in Shell-Mex house, next to the Savoy Hotel on the Thames Embankment. Immediately after the jolt he heard a second sound, ignored by most Londoners: a heavy object rushing through the air, which would later be likened to a train passing overhead. This was the rumbling of the missile through the earth's atmosphere, on the way to impacting on its target; travelling several times faster than sound, it had outrun its own noise.

Sandys knew all too well what had caused the explosions. He also realised that his words about the Battle of London being over had been spoken much too soon.

At his home in The Hague, Holland, 14-year-old Hans van Wouw Koeleman heard a different kind of sound. The Hague lies less than 200 miles east of London, but Hans was enjoying 'a beautiful sunny day', made even sunnier by the fact that there was no school. When an unusually loud roar flooded his house, young Hans thought was some new kind of German or Allied plane and ran outside to take a look.

Instead of aeroplanes, Hans spotted the long shapes of two A-4 long-range rockets rising straight up, 'just before they hit the cold air and the contrails were formed'. Both were launched simultaneously from Wassenaar, just north-east of The Hague, by 485 (Mobile) Artillery detachment. Hans recalls that 'the thunder of the rocket engines was tremendous'.

The double launching took place at 6.39 (London time). Only five minutes would pass before the first rocket slammed into Staveley Road, Chiswick, travelling at nearly 5,000 miles per hour.

Although the rocket attack had finally begun, the worries of the launching crews were far from over. Fuel and supplies, especially the highly volatile liquid oxygen, were being brought in from Germany in frustratingly small amounts. The rockets themselves were another headache. By the time they reached their launching

'... about 30 feet wide and 10 feet deep.' This (blemished) photograph shows a typical crater made by a V-2 rocket. Houses near the crater have been demolished, but damage from the blast carried right down both sides of the street. The explosion was originally blamed on an 'unknown' missile.

sites, more than half were not fit for firing.

Over-long storage was causing the inner workings of many missiles to waste away. After the rockets left the giant underground Central Works factory at Nordhausen, they were stockpiled in depots along the north-western border. There they remained, for weeks at a time.

When they were finally turned over to the launching crews, a large percentage of the A-4s were found to be in poor condition. Vital components had corroded away; electrical systems were especially vulnerable, and were usually the first to go. After the wiring started to rot, the 46 foot-long missiles became useless piles of scrap metal.

The Allied armies were another major worry. American, British, and Canadian troops were already into Belgium and at the German border. Each battery commander was advised to be ready to move out of their areas within a few hours' notice – in case of a new Allied offensive, SS General Hans Kammler, commander of all the rocket units, did not want the missiles to fall into enemy hands.

The commander of 444 (Training and Experimental) Battery had already been ordered to withdraw from the German town of Euskirchen, which was too close to the Belgian border for comfort. After launching a single rocket at Paris on 8th September, the men of 444 Battery took their three mobile launching platforms to the island of Walchern in western Holland. On Walchern Island, the battery would not only be out of reach in case of an Allied advance, but would also be in position to begin firing on London.

At The Hague, 485 (Mobile) Artillery Detachment's nine launching crews waited to see what would happen next. Their orders were to keep firing at London, but the Detachment also was on alert for a possible pull-out to the east. No one was sure if they should continue with launching preparations, or shut down and withdraw into Germany.

No one in Winston Churchill's War Cabinet knew what to do, either. The V-2 attack had come as a very nasty shock. Everyone had hoped that the air strikes against Peenemünde and other rocket targets had stopped the missiles, or that the drive into the Low Countries had pushed them out of range. But all the planning,

DAVID JOHNSON

A V-2's flight from The Hague to London, just under 200 miles, took about four minutes. The rocket travelled through the stratosphere with the speed of a rifle bullet, reaching a maximum height of 55-60 miles.

intelligence work and air activity had gone for nothing.

One or two Cabinet members were not alarmed by the rocket's arrival. The V-2's one-ton warhead was far too small to worry about, the sceptics argued. An old twin-engined Heinkel He111 bomber could deliver a larger payload with a lot less bother and expense.

But Duncan Sandys realised the one great difference between the Heinkel He111 and the V-2: the bomber could be shot down, but there was no defence against the rocket. And, as everyone would soon find out, the missile's warhead – as large and every bit as potent as the Flying Bomb's – was nothing to be scoffed at.

CHAPTER SEVEN

'Gas Mains' and 'Phantom Bangs'

'To see one of them lift off was a majestic sight,' recalls Hans van Wouw Koeleman. 'A huge torpedo, sometimes all aluminium, sometimes painted black and white or red and white, slowly rising on a tail of fire.'

From his home in The Hague, young Hans saw quite a few V-2s blast off. Watching the tall missiles roar off their firing tables was an awe-inspiring experience for onlookers. But to the launching unit's technicians and engineers, preparing an A-4 for firing meant hard work and tense nerves. An A-4 was such a sophisticated weapon that even the smallest error might cause it to malfunction and crash, or blow up on the ground.

Before the launching procedure began the A-4, laid out full-length on a *Meillerwagen* trailer, was rolled up to its launch site. The unique *Meillerwagen* not only transported the missile to its site, but also raised it to a vertical firing position and served as a firing platform.

At the launching site – any level surface would support a lift-off, even a roadway or a clearing in the woods – the *Meillerwagen*'s hydraulic lifting pistons were activated and the missile was slowly raised to its vertical position. Shifting the rocket, pushing it from its resting state on the trailer until its nose pointed straight up, took about fifteen minutes.

Once it was in launching position, all electrical cables were connected up and tests on circuits and systems were carried out. Next, the liquid oxygen and alcohol tanks rolled up to begin fuelling the 46-foot missile. Everything was designed with mobility in mind; not only were the tankers on wheels, but were also made of a light-weight aluminium alloy.

After both tanks were filled there were still several other operations to perform, including activating the rocket's gyroscope mechanism. When these tasks were done, the *Meillerwagen* was moved away from the rocket, lowered to its horizontal position – it had been serving as a gantry tower during the testing and fuelling – and wheeled away from the firing area.

Just over an hour after the missile arrived at its launching site, its firing table was given one last check to make sure it was level. One final job still remained; the crew installed the rocket's electronic ignition. Then a terse announcement came from the command trailer: 'X minus three minutes. Counting down.'

Three minutes remained before launching time. Except for the unit commander and a few technicians, who were already inside the armoured trailer, everyone took shelter in a hastily dug slit trench. All eyes kept a steady watch on the gleaming 46 foot-high missile during those three tense minutes – 'Peenemünde minutes' General Dornberger called them, which seemed ten times longer than only sixty seconds.

Rising smoothly to a sharp point, the rocket had a gracefulness and an almost hypnotic appeal not usually found in weapons of war. Each of its four fins was lacquered a different colour, as an aid to observation, and the body was painted an eye-catching black-and-white square pattern. Vapour from the liquid oxygen tank streamed out of the vents, giving the rocket a slightly ethereal aura.

At 'X minus one minute' technicians in the command trailer closed these vents, abruptly stopping the white oxygen vapour. A green warning flare arched into the air as the countdown entered its final ten seconds, a routine but unnecessary precaution since the crew members had already taken cover.

Inside the trailer, the commander peered through the narrow observation slits for the last few seconds before finally giving the order, 'Ignition!' Sitting an arm's length away from the officer, facing a panel of switches and gauges, the propulsion engineer pushed the first of three buttons. While everyone looked on, the rocket's tail burst into a stream of sparks that glanced off the launching stand's blast deflector and bounced wildly in all directions.

The sparks quickly became a steady cascade of red-yellow flame, which shot out of the missile's stern at an initial thrust of eight tons. Odds and ends of debris were blown clear of the launching platform and flew high into the air, propelled hundreds of feet by the engine blast.

By pushing a second button, the rocket was switched over from the outside generators to its own batteries for running the gyro-compass and guidance system. The propulsion engineer then pushed the third and final switch of the series, activating a turbo-pump that fed 33 gallons of alcohol and liquid oxygen per second into the rocket engine's combustion chamber. After about one second, the engine's thrust rose to twenty-five tons.

With agonising slowness the tall, shiny object began rising straight off its launching platform, obscuring both the platform and itself in a cloud of dust and smoke. Everyone gazed at the spectacle in awed silence, overwhelmed by the display. It was a sight that no one ever tired of watching, no matter how many launches or test shots they might have seen before.

Lift-off was sluggish, as though the machine was being hoisted by pulleys, but the missile's speed increased as it gained altitude – slowly at first, then noticeably faster, while the sunlight reflected off its bright glazing. After it had risen a few hundred feet, the flame from its tail became as long as the rocket itself.

Four and a half seconds after launching, the pointed nose began to tilt westward, on its way to London. As the steady roar moved farther off, other sounds could be heard – the timekeeper marking off the seconds of flight, and even the wind rustling through the trees, which sounded strangely hollow to the ear after the engine's blast.

The rumble continued to grow fainter and farther away. After about 23 seconds the missile reached 'sonic velocity' – it was now travelling faster than sound – but still remained clearly visible through binoculars. Its long, vivid tail marked the spot as it roared toward the upper atmosphere.

Twelve seconds afterwards the rocket was six miles above the earth's surface, travelling at twice the speed of sound. By this time it was only a foreshortened speck in the observers' glasses, but could still be quickly spotted by the white streak of vapourised liquid oxygen trailing behind it. As altitude continued to increase the

'… the *Meillerwagen* was moved away from the rocket …' A *Meillerwagen* trailer in the raised position. Note the hydraulic pistons for lifting the framework, along with a cradled A-4 rocket, into firing position. Also note the trees in the background which provided natural camouflage for the launch.

'... there were still several other operations to perform, including activating the rocket's gyroscope mechanism.' A technician, standing on the *Meillerwagen*'s framework, adjusts the gyroscope just prior to launch.

layers of air made the vapour trail appear as a zig-zag, a phenomenon known as 'frozen lightning'.

The bright yellow flame suddenly vanished at about fifty-four seconds after launch, and a voice from the command trailer called, 'All burnt!' Empty of fuel, the rocket streaked through the stratosphere at 3,200 feet per second – a higher velocity than most rifle bullets.

After the 'All burnt' signal, the unit commander and his propulsion officer exchanged a short, silent handshake. The time-keeper also got in on the handshaking, but not before carefully noting the time of lift-off, 'All burnt' time, and calculating the moment of impact.

In just over four minutes after the flame had abruptly gone out, the rocket would crash into the largest and most crowded city in Britain. General Walter Dornberger estimated that the impact would have the force of 50 railway locomotives, each weighing 100 tons, slamming into London at 60 miles per hour. After impact, the rocket's one ton warhead, filled with Trialen, would add to the havoc, blasting everything within a quarter-mile radius.

Between 8th and 18th September 1944 only 25 rockets fell on Britain. Most were fired from The Hague by 485 (Mobile) Artillery Detachment. After 14th September, 444 Battery also began firing from Walchern Island.

Every shot was aimed at London, but only 16 of the 25 actually hit the target. The other nine landed on the surrounding counties. Casualties had been light; so far, fewer than 50 people had been killed.

Luck was largely responsible for the low death toll. Most of the missiles hit areas that were either lightly populated or not inhabited at all. One exploded after burying itself into a mud flat in Kent.

Another factor was the low rate of fire, caused by the large number of faulty rockets. More A-4 rockets were being shipped back to Germany as scrap, usually because of corroded electrical systems, than were being launched at Britain. Unreliable shipments of fuel and supplies also helped to cut down on the number of shots.

'The missile's speed increased as it gained altitude ...' A V-2 rocket lifts slowly from its test stand at Peenemünde. The black and white squares aided spotters in observing any roll or pitch by the missile, which was always called the A-4 by technicians.

'... 33 gallons of alcohol and liquid oxygen per second' were transformed into 25 tons of thrust in the A-4 rocket's combustion chamber. This photo was taken at the Central Works factory at Nordhausen, which was built underneath the Harz Mountains.

In London, most people still had not seen any damage caused by the rockets. Even though the explosion carried for miles each time a missile struck, people could only guess at what was happening. Newspapers were forced to ignore the loud booms that suddenly rattled windows at odd times throughout the day; even hinting at the existence of the German rockets was strictly forbidden by the once again strictly enforced censorship laws.

British Intelligence coined the code-name 'Big Ben' for the guided missile. On 8th September, the day of the Staveley Road incident, this notice was issued by Intelligence, stamped 'SECRET':

> It has been decided that the special security measures for which the signal BIG BEN CONFIRMED was devised will not be taken for the present, and accordingly BIG BEN CONFIRMED has not yet been issued.

The government refused to confirm any suspicions about the rocket attack, and the security lid was on.

Although there was no official news, rumours about the mysterious explosions flew left and right. Some people remembered the brief news columns of a few weeks before that mentioned the 'V-2' and quickly put two and two together. But few knew anything for sure.

Every explanation from radio-controlled German time bombs to exploding gas mains was given – the government did not issue the 'gas main' reports, but did not deny them, either. A woman in the Notting Hill district of London felt positive that these were no gas works explosions – sixteen gas mains in ten days was rather a lot, even for people who didn't keep an actual count. It had to be something the Germans were sending over.

The big bangs were *the* topic of conversation, just as the Flying Bombs had been two months before. Stories were constantly being made up about the new weapon; a new one was heard almost every day. It was rumoured that a terrible new kind of explosive was being used; that the warhead of this secret bomb weighed 20 tons; that craters from the blast were a quarter of a mile across.

But even those with 'inside' information got the facts wrong sometimes, just as they had with the doodlebugs. Richard Baker of US Intelligence tried to find out a thing or two from a man named

Sam Welles, who was a special assistant to US Ambassador John G. Winant. Welles informed Baker that the recent booms were caused by 1,100-lb rocket bombs (warhead weight off by 1,000 lbs) that plummeted to earth from a height of 15 miles (actual height about 55 miles).

'People are saying that these big explosions are caused by the threatened new rocket-bomb called V-2,' commented Hilda Neal on 13th September – the day after a rocket destroyed the Chrysler plant at Mortlake, in south-east London.

'Another very loud bang this morning,' Miss Neal reported next day. That rocket hit Leytonstone, in north-east London, nine miles away from Hilda Neal's flat, but the blast was still strong enough to give her a shock. 'As we are ten miles inside Germany,' Miss Neal went on, 'the public is counting on the war ending very soon now ...'

The public certainly was counting on the war ending very soon. London was still riding the crest of the wave. After the drive across France in August, everyone was sure that the Allied armies would simply overrun the places from which the secret weapons were being launched. Just 'one more big push,' like in August, and it would all be over.

What the public did not know was that the armies still were in no condition to make any kind of push. The supply problem in France was worse than ever; getting men and equipment to the front was still the big worry. Correcting the supply situation was going to take longer than anyone expected.

In their retreat into Germany, the Wehrmacht destroyed much of northern France's railway system. British and American air raids added their share of damage. Because the railways were in such a shambles, all supplies had to be transported by road, which meant smaller shipments and slower travelling.

Even though the roads north of Paris were packed with lines of olive-drab army vehicles, it would take several more weeks before enough ammunition, food, spare parts, and other vital equipment could be stockpiled near the German border. By that time, bad weather might be causing still more problems.

But London knew nothing about supplies, and cared even less. People only knew what they had been told, and lately the news could not have been better: Allied troops were facing the Siegfried Line, inside Germany's borders; the government had ended the evacuation of London; it had been officially announced that 'The Battle of London is over'. As far as many Londoners were concerned, the war was as good as won already.

Over one million people had left the city because of the Flying Bombs during June, July, and August. After Herbert Morrison's evacuation announcement on 7th September, the 'buzz bomb refugees' began coming back into London at the rate of 10,000 every week.

Government officials were alarmed about the returning crowds, but could not warn them to stay away; because no mention of the rockets was allowed, no warning could be given. Newspapers and radio announcements issued false reports on an expected new wave of Flying Bombs or exaggerated about the lack of housing space, all in an attempt to frighten people away from London, but none of this seemed to have any effect. Trainloads of women and children kept arriving every hour; every one of the refugees carried large bundles and bulging suitcases.

American Navy Yeoman Don Cumming commented, 'It amused me no end to read the frantic efforts of the newspapers to keep these people out of the city, using all sorts of excuses ... but never mentioning the stern fact that the rocket attack had begun.'

While civil authorities worried about civilians returning to the V-2 target area, the Allied Expeditionary Air Force had its own hands full. Just trying to find out where the rockets were coming from was a full-time job.

In an attempt to locate the launching sites, radar stations along the east coast of England kept a special watch. Mobile radar platforms also were moved into position, and even observation balloons were used. The rockets did leave a trace on radar screens, especially just after lift-off when the missiles were still relatively slow-moving. But the blips were too brief and imprecise to locate the launch areas.

Reports from the Dutch underground gave British Intelligence its first solid clue. An A-4 rocket rising under 25 tons of thrust could be seen and heard by Dutch civilians a mile away. Members of the underground took special note of what they saw and heard, and sent reports of their observations to London.

Quite a few of the launchings took place in the *Speergebiet*, a two-mile strip of land along the Dutch coast from which all residents had been forced to leave. Security measures along this strip were fairly strict – the Germans wanted no prying eyes to see how their rockets were set-up and launched – but civilians still managed to get close enough for a good look.

Because he was only 14 years old, Hans van Wouw Koeleman was free to go in and out of the restricted area. He always took a small, hand-built push cart for carrying firewood, and could go into the *Speergebiet* without being bothered.

Once inside the restricted zone, however, Hans did more than just chop kindling. He and his friends got to know some of the German soldiers; they would strike up conversations with the grey-uniformed men and found out 'a lot of gratuitous data'.

Hans also saw a few actual launchings from close up. While hidden in the bushes, he observed one launch from a distance of about 1,000 metres. More than 35 years later, he can still feel the heat on his face from the rocket's ignition and lift-off.

When he returned from the *Speergebiet*, Hans would report his observations to a Swiss girl that he knew. The girl was part of a courier system that, among other things, delivered a news sheet, an illegal paper made up from items heard on BBC radio broadcasts. As a neutral citizen, she had the necessary *Ausweise* (permits) for moving about the area, and had much more freedom than any Dutch civilian. Hans never found out what she did with the information he gave her.

In London, Duncan Sandys and the other rocket experts still had quite a lot to learn themselves. One thing that nobody seemed to realise was that the missiles were being launched from the free-wheeling *Meillerwagen* trailers. A lot of time was wasted while trying to locate non-existent launching tables, which were supposed to look like 'lemon squeezers'.

Actually, the firing tables were attached right to the *Meillerwagen*, and were not lowered onto the ground until the missile was hoisted into firing position. After the launch, it was picked up again and wheeled away.

A tree-lined street, such as the Rijks Straatsweg which runs north from The Hague through Wassenaar, was the ideal launching site – it was firm and level, accessible to all launch vehicles, and the tall trees provided natural camouflage for the 46 foot-high rockets. The *Haagsche Bosch*, a forested park inside The Hague, was another favourite launching ground.

All traffic would be cleared from the selected roadway just before launch. In just over an hour later, after firing, crew members lowered the *Meillerwagen*'s gantry tower, packed their gear, and drove off. If any Allied fighters arrived, they found nothing at all.

It took Intelligence quite a while before they found out how movable the new rockets were, which came as no good news. Not only was the rocket impossible to stop after firing, but was also going to be a major headache to stop on the ground.

Both the RAF and the US Army Air Force did their best to stop the missiles. In September, the US Eighth Air Force sent more than 100 fighters over Belgium and Holland to strafe anything that looked like a target. The fighter sweep shot up a lot of vehicles and railway cars, and probably was at least partly responsible for the shortage of liquid oxygen and other supplies at the A-4 launch sites.

Some rocket experts in Britain came up with the idea of tampering with the radio beams that (they thought) guided the rockets. If they had been right, this would have deflected the missiles before they reached London. But since the A-4 had no radio-control mechanism, the plan came to nothing.

'Every day we wait and hope for something that will end these phantom bangs.' This was written by a man in Leytonstone after a rocket hit the district on 14th September, but the words might have come from almost any member of Winston Churchill's War Cabinet. Now that the missiles were being fired at London, all that anyone in the Cabinet could do was to stay informed of all the steps taken to combat the long-range missiles and, like everybody in London, keep waiting and hoping.

CHAPTER EIGHT

'Well, That Seems To Be That'

General Dwight D. Eisenhower could not help showing his anger. The Supreme Commander of the Allied Forces was usually the most easy-going of men, but he had just finished reading a communiqué that really set him off. The message was from Field Marshal Bernard Montgomery concerning a plan for 'winning the war' – a plan that had already been rejected three times. After reading the message, Eisenhower verbally blasted Montgomery, his fantastic ideas, and the Field Marshal's irritating persistence.

Since mid-August, Montgomery had been proposing what he called his 'single-thrust plan' – an idea for sending one powerful drive across the Rhine River and then straight on to Berlin, ending the war in 1944. The Field Marshal openly disagreed with Eisenhower's 'broad-front policy' – advancing toward the German border with several separate drives, which had been the strategy during the July and August dash through France.

Montgomery's 'single-thrust plan' had been considered before, but General Eisenhower decided that it was too risky. It might be a quick success, as the Field Marshal said, but it might also turn into a disaster. Eisenhower did not want to take the risk.

General Eisenhower not only disliked Montgomery's plan, but he did not think very highly of Montgomery, either. He considered the Field Marshal an overbearing egomaniac, who always went out of his way to prove himself right and everybody else wrong. This latest message served to confirm Eisenhower's opinion.

The way the Supreme Commander saw it, activating the Belgian port of Antwerp had top priority, not gambling on some drive across the Rhine. Antwerp, with its three miles of wharves, was indispensable for untangling the Allied supply problem. If

American and British freighters were able to unload their cargoes at the deep-water harbour, it would no longer be necessary to transport everything 450 miles from Cherbourg.

But Antwerp lay 54 miles from the sea; before any ships could reach the unloading docks, they had to pass through the harbour's long and narrow seaward approaches. And the land on both sides of this channel, including Walchern Island was still in the hands of the Wehrmacht. Even though the town of Antwerp was held by British troops, no Allied shipping could reach the docks.

One of General Eisenhower's most important problems was rooting the enemy out of Antwerp's approaches, and giving the Allied armies a major port right at the front line. He did not feel much like listening to another one of Montgomery's self-serving lectures on strategy and tactics.

Although he personally disliked Montgomery, Eisenhower did not want an open feud with the Field Marshal for Montgomery, the hero of El Alamein, was one of the most popular men in Britain. A quarrel might put a heavy strain on relations between Britain and America. So Eisenhower agreed to meet with Montgomery and, he hoped, straighten out the Field Marshal once and for all.

On Sunday, 10th September, General Eisenhower flew to Brussels for the meeting with Field Marshal Montgomery. Eisenhower wrenched his knee a week earlier and could not leave the plane, so the conference was held on board. No sooner had Montgomery arrived than he began railing against the current Allied strategy and promoting his own plan for a single push across the Rhine.

The Field Marshal came up with the same arguments. If he were given all the men and equipment he asked for, Montgomery insisted, he could capture a bridge across the Rhine and be in Berlin before New Year. But aside from all the bluster and bombast, Montgomery also had a new line of persuasion.

Since 8th September, the Field Marshal pointed out, the German V-2 rockets had been in operation. Intelligence knew that the missiles were being launched from somewhere in western Holland. The 'single-thrust plan' that he was proposing would not only secure a springboard into Germany but, if it succeeded, would also neutralise the rocket threat.

As Supreme Commander of all Allied Forces, General Dwight D. Eisenhower was ultimately responsible for all ground and air operations against the German secret weapons.

Montgomery wanted to drop three airborne divisions – the British 1st Airborne, the American 82nd and 101st Divisions, as well as the Polish 1st Parachute Brigade – north of the Dutch town of Arnhem. The objective of the paratroops would be the Lower Rhine bridge that connected the northern and southern halves of the town. After the bridge had been captured, British armoured units would rush north from the front lines, dash across the Arnhem bridge, and wheel into the Ruhr Valley.

In one stroke, Germany's natural defensive barrier, the Rhine, would be crossed and the Siegfried Line defences outflanked. Also, supply routes from Germany to the V-2 sites would be cut off. Once the launch area was isolated, the sites could be overrun and the launching units captured, just like the Flying Bomb ramps had been captured in the Pas de Calais.

The plan would be christened 'Operation Market-Garden'. 'Market' indicated the airborne part of the operation, and 'Garden' the armoured drive to the north.

General Eisenhower listened carefully to the Field Marshal, and was impressed by what he heard. Eisenhower realised that the summer offensive had all but petered out; Market-Garden could start it up again. Also, the new guided missiles had to be taken care of. Montgomery's plan might solve both problems at once.

Although he was certain that Montgomery was a bit too optimistic about the Arnhem operation – it probably would not put the Allies in Berlin by the year's end – Eisenhower not only approved of the plan, but gave it top priority, insisting that it start as soon as possible. If Operation Market-Garden succeeded in capturing the Arnhem bridge, he would take things from there. But the airdrop was well worth the risk, especially since the V-2 rocket attack had begun.

General Eisenhower might not have been all that hopeful, but most Londoners thought that the fighting was going into its last days. The rockets, or gas mains, or whatever they were amounted to nothing more than a nuisance so far. After the July and August advances across France, everybody was sure that the Wehrmacht was finished.

A few days after Montgomery met Eisenhower, Richard Baker

had another talk with Sam Welles, the special assistant to the American ambassador. Welles thought that the war would end by November at the latest. The Germans had not been able to stage any kind of counter-offensive, despite over-extended Allied supply lines, and a new Russian drive was expected on the Eastern Front.

There were other signs of confidence as well. Some London shops were selling red, white, and blue streamers for Victory Day. In the block of flats where Richard Baker lived, two statues were brought up from the cellar, where they had been placed for protection during the Blitz, and returned to their niches in the entrance hall.

The German High Command had no intention of conceding defeat, however. After the German divisions had withdrawn behind the Siegfried Line defences, they would be regrouped and turned against the advancing Allied armies. Morale in many Wehrmacht and Panzer units was surprisingly high in spite of the six week retreat. Now that they were on German soil, the troops were more determined than ever to give the enemy a hard, bitter fight.

Adolf Hitler seemed more concerned with the attack on London than with Allied moves in France and the Low Countries. He was delighted that the new rockets – now officially being called 'V-2' even though the launch crews still referred to the missile as the A-4 – were hitting London. Hitler was concerned with the slow rate of fire, however, and asked Munitions Minister Albert Speer what to do about it.

Albert Speer's first thought was to increase production. German industry, under constant attack from British and American bombers, could not turn out both the rocket and the Flying Bomb. Since the Flying Bombs were no longer effective for attacks against London, they would be dropped far down on the priorities list in favour of the V-2.

From September onward, the number of rockets coming out of the underground factories at Nordhausen increased while Flying Bomb production would drop. Over 600 A-4 missiles were produced by the Central Works in September and, under Albert Speer's energy, would continue to top the 600 mark in the coming months.

People stopped where they were, on the street or in their back gardens, to stare up at the spectacle passing overhead. Bus riders in Essex and Kent craned their necks to get a glimpse of the row upon row of aircraft, which made the most incredible ear-shattering racket as they droned across the sky.

Sunday, 17th September 1944 was 'Battle of Britain Sunday'. All over England, special church services were being held to commemorate the RAF's decisive victory over the Luftwaffe in 1940. The colossal din, made by the heaviest air traffic that anyone could remember, broke up quite a few of the services, including the Mass at Westminster Cathedral in London.

Crowds began to gather on the streets, hypnotised by the sight and the roaring engines of more aircraft than they had ever seen. A boy in East London watched the procession from his bedroom window – which was minus its glass thanks to a nearby Flying Bomb explosion – and then ran over to scribble in his diary, 'Planes and more planes – there must be thousands of them.'

In The Hague, Holland, 14-year-old Hans van Wouw Koeleman also saw and heard them. There were aircraft of every size and description – twin-engine C-47 transports and four-engine Stirling bombers, towing small Horsa and Waco gliders, all flying in rigid formation. Darting protectively around the transports were British Spitfires and Typhoons and American P-51 Mustangs, P-38 Lightnings, and P-47 Thunderbolts.

Altogether, there were 4,700 aeroplanes, over 2,000 of them troop-carrying planes, churning their way to the drop zones in Holland. It was the largest airborne force ever launched, carrying 35,000 men: 24,000 of them would land by parachute, 11,000 would come down in the long, flat-sided gliders. Anyone who saw them ploughing through the bright morning sky was convinced that nothing could stand in the way of such a mighty enterprise. Hans van Wouw Koeleman thought the paratroops 'had come to liberate us'.

The air drop near the town of Arnhem went according to plan, even though heavy anti-aircraft fire took its toll of the slow troop-carrying planes. But almost immediately after the gliders and paratroops landed, the Market-Garden campaign began falling behind schedule, deadly to such an operation, which depended upon quick and precise movements. Also, by the sheerest co-

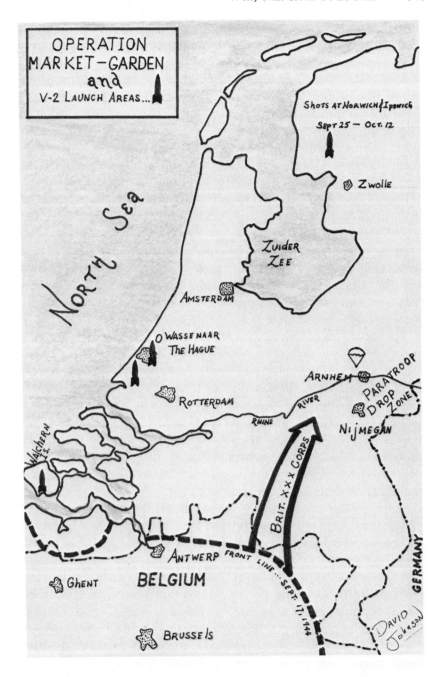

incidence, two SS armoured units, including a full Panzer division, were in the Arnhem area on 17th September. The airborne force landed practically right on top of them.

As the day wore on, luck continued to turn against the Allied troops. Resistance from German forces was heavy, pinning down the paratroop units for critical intervals. Communications between British and American detachments, essential for co-ordinating the attack, broke down.

By a freak accident, a briefcase containing all the plans for the operation – units involved, locations of drop zones, landing times – fell into German hands. Every mounting setback gnawed away at the exactly planned attack. By the second day of the battle, a crisis was already at hand.

In London, the public remained blissfully unaware of the setbacks in Holland. News reports were sketchy but encouraging. The 'big push' that everyone hoped for had come at last; people had seen it with their own eyes. The feeling was still that the end of the war was only a short way off.

The headlines of London's *News Chronicle* announced, 'AIR ARMY SEIZES TOWNS IN HOLLAND' in its 18th September edition. Other reports were just as vague. Not until 21st September did the papers begin to hint that all was not well. 'STIFFEST FIGHTING SINCE CAEN' warned the *News Chronicle* on the 21st, referring to the drawn-out battle near the Norman town of Caen during June and July.

One part of Operation Market-Garden had already failed. The rocket launching units, which General Eisenhower and Field Marshal Montgomery were hoping to isolate and capture, had pulled out of their firing areas at The Hague and Walchern Island. As soon as the paratroops began to land, the rockets and their crews were ordered to withdraw into Germany and northern Holland by SS Major General Hans Kammler, the man in charge of the V-2 attack.

Allied planners still failed to realise that the rocket units were completely mobile. The Flying Bombs had been fired from fixed ramps so, Intelligence reasoned, the missiles must also be launched from fixed emplacements. The *Meillerwagen* was still undiscovered. It would take a while before Intelligence learned the truth, the hard way.

From their new launching ground near Zwolle, Holland, the rocket units began firing at the East Anglian towns of Ipswich and Norwich. No major damage was done to either city; only 35 missiles were fired from Zwolle. The rocket batteries would head back to The Hague as quickly as possible but, meanwhile, as long as London was out of range, any British target was better than none.

For five days, Operation Market-Garden struggled against mounting losses and almost constant enemy attacks. The Battle for the Bridgehead across the Rhine ground down to a fight for survival that quickly became a losing fight.

Bad weather over England slowed the arrival of reinforcements on 18th September. On the 21st a Polish parachute brigade, sent in to bolster the troops fighting inside Arnhem, were blocked by a German force. Next day, the British armoured drive toward the bridge was cut off by a German counter-attack.

Defeat was finally acknowledged on 26th September. Only nine days after the engines of 4,700 aircraft shook the windows of south-eastern England, filling each eyewitness with hope and enthusiasm, the Allied forces were ordered to withdraw from Arnhem.

In the nine days during the Battle of Arnhem, Allied casualties numbered over 17,000, 5,000 more than in the D-Day landings. Although Field Marshal Montgomery would claim that the assault was '90 per cent successful', the bridge across the Rhine at Arnhem was still held by the enemy.

In London, the press was not given the green light to publish the bad news until the 28th, two days after the evacuation began.

ARNHEM: AIR TROOPS WITHDRAWN
STORY OF 9 HEROIC DAYS

Headlines tried not to sound too pessimistic, but there was little anyone could say or do to brighten a major defeat.

Most Londoners did not grasp the strategic fine points of Operation Market-Garden or its failure. But the setback did bring home one brutal fact – the German army was nowhere near the verge of collapse, as everyone had been told, and the war would definitely not be over by Christmas.

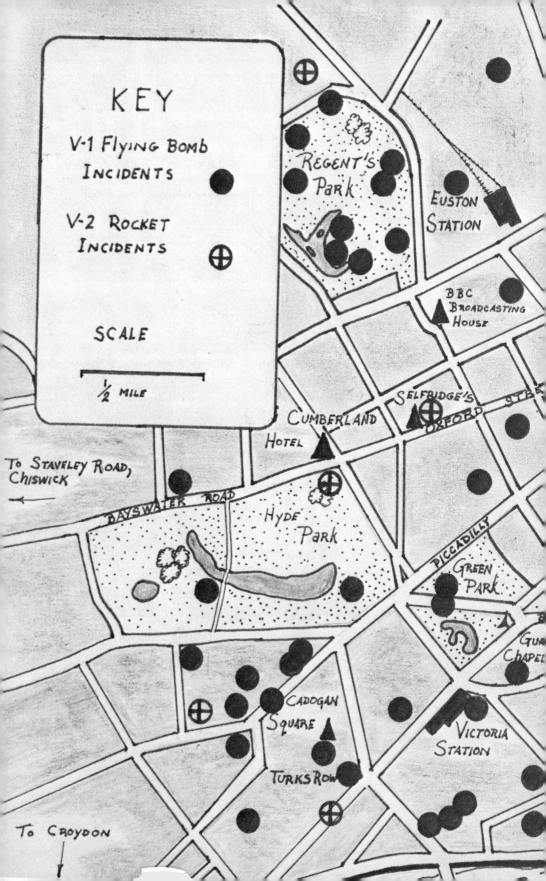

KEY

V-1 FLYING BOMB
   INCIDENTS   ●

V-2 ROCKET
   INCIDENTS   ⊕

SCALE

½ MILE

REGENT'S
Park

EUSTON
Station

BBC
BROADCASTING
House

SELFRIDGE'S OXFORD STRE

CUMBERLAND
Hotel

To STAVELEY ROAD,
Chiswick

BAYSWATER ROAD

Hyde
Park

PICCADILLY

GREEN
Park

GUA
Chapel

CADOGAN
Square

VICTORIA
Station

TURKS ROW

To CROYDON

V-1 AND V-2 INCIDENTS IN CENTRAL LONDON

MAP by DAVID JOHNSON

Just two weeks after Richard Baker heard the fighting would be over by November, he underwent a complete change of heart – he could no longer believe that the war would end before the spring of 1945. Near Victoria Station, two men in dark business suits stood silently reading their papers in front of a news stand. As they scanned the front page story about Arnhem, one of the men glanced up and said to no one in particular, 'Well, that seems to be that.'

In the weeks to come, London would be in for a lot more bad news. The V-2 threat was still alive and well. A week after the pullout from Arnhem, General Kammler's rocket launching units, both 485 Detachment and 444 Battery, were back in The Hague. On 3rd October the missile attack on London started where it had left off.

CHAPTER NINE

'Poor London. Poor Me.'

The nine o'clock news was always a nightly event – even though the radio broadcasts were hardly ever as colourful as the neighbour's latest rumour – and news vendors never had any trouble getting rid of their flimsy four page papers. Every word about the fighting 'across the Channel' was absorbed quickly and completely. But Londoners had their own struggle to get through every day, less dramatic but just as grim – a struggle with the butcher, the grocer, and the ration books.

Food wasn't nearly as scarce as it had been in 1942 and 1943, when German U-Boats torpedoed hundreds of merchant ships in mid-Atlantic. But rations were still dull and far from plentiful. The constant wartime complaint of 'feeling tired all the time' was mainly because of poor diet.

After undressing for bed one night, Richard Baker of US Intelligence caught sight of himself in a full-length mirror. Baker could not believe how much weight he had lost in the five months since leaving the United States, and was astonished to see how far his ribs stuck out. And at the US mess hall Baker got more and better food – citrus fruits, milk, eggs – than any Londoner.

To Gwladys Cox of West Hampstead, the scarcity of food was not nearly as bad as the monotony of the restricted diet. Mrs Cox and her husband Ralph existed mainly on the none-too-flavourful wartime sausages; they were filled mostly with bread and were so dry that American GIs called them 'sawdust rolls' (among other things). A typical lunch at the Coxes': sausages, powdered egg omelette, and potatoes. One woman in south London found at least one good thing about the awful food – it helped take her mind off the unexplained *booms*.

Food was not the only thing that was rationed; clothing and all manner of things were hard to come by. The public had been told to 'make do and mend'. Because of rationing, most suits and overcoats seen on the street were frayed and tattered. The diary of a young woman from Wimbledon, south London complains:

> Everything in the house is worn out. There are no new curtains or covers because the prices are outrageous – besides, we can't afford the coupons. Stair carpets are threadbare. Everything needs painting, inside and out. My wardrobe is an unholy mess – the only decent dresses I have are over five years old. The only comfort I have is that every other house is just as dreary looking, and everybody else's clothes are in worse condition than mine. Poor London. Poor Me.

The evacuation of over a million people during the Flying Bombs made things much more plentiful. Everything from fresh milk to copies of *The Times* were available. But now that the evacuees were coming back, food and all other items once again became scarce.

During the Blitz in 1940 and 1941, most of the West End theatres stayed closed. But both theatres and cinemas stayed open for business while the buzz bombs and rockets came over. If the sirens sounded during a performance, an 'Air Raid' sign was flashed, allowing nervous members of the audience to leave for the nearest shelter. Few people ever left during an Alert.

A few shows folded during the Flying Bombs, and attendance did suffer. *There Shall Be No Night* with Alfred Lunt and Lynn Fontanne closed when the Aldwych Theatre was badly damaged on 30th June; the theatre was blasted by the same bomb that hit the Air Ministry building. But by mid-October, thirty theatres were open. The Old Vic was presenting Laurence Olivier and Ralph Richardson in *Richard III* at the New (now the Albery) Theatre.

Filmgoers had nothing as grand as this, but they had their excitement just the same. *The Hitler Gang* was playing all over London, billed as 'The Greatest Gangster Picture of them All'.

Even though London was still under attack, and looked it, some signs of the war were already starting to disappear. On 17th September, the same day as the massive paratroop assault at Arnhem, the blackout officially ended. It was replaced by 'half-lighting', or the Dimout.

The blackout had gone into effect on the first night of the war, 3rd September 1939. At first, the complete lack of outdoor lighting – neon signs, window lights, street lights – caused an alarming rash of deaths and injuries on the roads. But by 1944 just about everyone except for a few American servicemen had adjusted to it, although people still injured themselves by walking into trees and lamp poles.

If anyone expected an instant transformation from total blackness to full illumination in one night, however, they were soon sadly disappointed. 'Well, when the night came there was some relaxation,' an air raid warden from London's Paddington district observed, 'but the dull glow that appeared from the windows ... failed to arouse any enthusiasm ... on the street.' While walking along Bond Street, Richard Baker noticed a pale glimmer coming from the street lamps. It was better than the blackout, he thought, but not much.

Some districts did not have the manpower to install new street globes. A good many people simply did not bother to remove their heavy blackout curtains. The drapes had been up for five years, accumulating a load of dirt and dead insects all the while; nobody was wild about facing such a clean-up task. Besides, most people only had one set of curtains, and the old habit of 'doing the blackout' would take quite a while to break.

On 14th November the Home Guard was ordered to stand down. A reserve unit made up of World War I veterans and those who were unfit for military service, the Home Guard was formed in 1940 during the German threat to invade England. Now, another sign of the war's 'winding down', the units were finally disbanded.

The government hoped that ending the blackout and dismissing the Home Guard would help boost morale. Instead, these actions had just the opposite effect.

In a West London borough's local newspaper, a one-column editorial expressed anger and frustration. The column blasted Duncan Sandys for his 'The Battle of London is over' announcement, which gave people a false sense of security. It went on to blame the lifting of the blackout and the Home Guard stand-down for adding to the deception, and criticised the government for encouraging evacuated mothers and children to return to London.

Coming after the heady days of the summer just past, when Allied troops seemed on the verge of marching straight to Berlin, the public mood certainly was glum. When the Home Guard was disbanded, a woman in south London worried that the move may have been 'premature'. 'The end of the European war, which in August seemed well in sight,' she wrote, 'now seems to have receded again.'

Government ministers were greatly concerned with the public's attitude, and with good reason. Morale was a lot more fragile than anyone was willing to admit. If confidence in the running of the war should vanish, it would be as crushing a defeat as any suffered on the battlefield.

An incident that took place in March 1943 brought home how frighteningly delicate morale could be. On the night of 3rd March 1943, an air raid Alert sounded. By the hundreds, people all over London began converging on air raid shelters – 'nervous and anxious to get under cover,' according to the official report – including the Underground station at Bethnal Green, East London.

Ten minutes after the sirens had gone, a salvo of 'Z' anti-aircraft rockets were fired about a third of a mile away from the Underground station. The rockets, streaking into the night air with a series of loud *zoooomms*, caused the uneasy crowd to panic. People began shoving their way down the dimly-lighted stairway to the train platform. A woman at the foot of the stairs fell, partly blocking the passage.

Within a matter of seconds, people were piled five, six, and more on top of one another. The crowd kept on pushing down. Hundreds were trapped by the crush. In the end, 173 people died – all from suffocation. Not an enemy bomb fell.

Herbert Morrison, the Minister of Home Security, tried to keep the incident quiet. But no such event can be kept secret; before long, the facts of the Bethnal Green Underground disaster were common knowledge.

So in July 1944 Morrison issued his own version of the incident. According to the Morrison report, the disaster had been caused by defects in the shelter; there was no question of any panic. Morrison feared that morale would take another nose dive if the truth were released.

But in the autumn of 1944, public opinion was sinking just the same. The Allied drive into Germany had stalled out; the Arnhem airdrop had been stopped in its tracks; and the 'flying gas mains' were no longer a joke.

Faith in Winston Churchill and his government was at a dangerously low point. The War Cabinet was doing nothing about the alarming blasts, which showed no signs of stopping. No one was even willing to say what was causing them.

LYRIC THEATRE

SHAFTESBURY AVENUE, W.I

THE YEARS BETWEEN
By DAPHNE DU MAURIER
HENRIETTA WATSON   ALLAN JEAYES

H. M. TENNENT LTD. and JOHN C. WILSON

present

LOVE IN IDLENESS

AIR-RAID WARNINGS
If a public air-raid warning is sounded in the course of a performance, the audience will be notified on the illuminated sign in front of the footlights for one minute. This does not necessarily mean that an air raid will take place, and we recommend you to remain in the theatre. If, however you wish to leave, you are at liberty to do so. All we ask is that, if you feel you must go, you will depart quietly, and, as far as possible, without disturbing others. The "Raiders Passed" signal will also be shown on the illuminated sign.

IMPORTANT NOTICE
During "Alerts" no trains run from Piccadilly Circus to Charing Cross, Waterloo, or Elephant; but there are special buses from Haymarket and Jermyn Street.

The Booking Hall, Piccadilly Circus Station, is NOT an air raid shelter. If you wish to take shelter, see list in Vestibule.

The air-raid warning included in a theatre programme for a play starring Alfred Lunt and Lynn Fontanne. Although attendance of films and theatre did suffer during the Flying Bomb and rocket attacks, those who went seldom left the theatre during an alert. (*Courtesy of Richard L. Temple*)

CHAPTER TEN

'A Different Ballgame'

Lieutenant Colonel Elwyn Righetti spotted the train from the cockpit of his P-51 Mustang fighter, 12,000 feet above southern Holland. A second later, his wingman's voice broke in over his headset, 'Do you see what I see?' It was a rhetorical question; Righetti was having a good look through his binoculars, and could see a big locomotive pulling a long line of freight cars. The procession was heading westward, toward the Dutch coast from the direction of the German border.

Colonel Righetti, commanding the US 338th Fighter Squadron, split the sixteen Mustangs into two groups. Four Mustangs would stay at 10,000 feet, flying 'top cover' in case any enemy fighters showed up. The others would go down 'on the deck' with him and give the train a working over.

After switching his gunsight on and charging the fighter's six .50 calibre machine guns, Righetti peeled off and dove straight for the target. He made his run-in from the side, planning on opening fire as the train passed in front of his guns. The altimeter read 1,200 feet when the locomotive entered his sights and Righetti pressed the firing button.

A handful of bursting stars flashed all over the locomotive and the cars just behind it – Righetti's armour-piercing incendiaries were finding their mark. When his wingman began firing, more of the brightly winking strikes rocked the steam engine in a dazzling display. The two silver and green Mustangs shot past the train before either pilot had the chance to check it for damage.

Colonel Righetti pulled up and the rest of the squadron began their strafing runs, two Mustangs at a time. He circled round for another firing pass, noticing that the locomotive was hardly moving; its bullet-punctured boiler threw off a dense cloud of steam.

On the next run-in, Righetti elected to make a head-on attack; this way, his guns would pass over the train's entire length. Once again, he peeled off into a fast, shallow dive and touched the firing button when the target came into range. The fighter shuddered as the six machine guns pounded, and hits darted along the chain of freight cars.

After pulling out, allowing the rest of the flight to go to work, Colonel Righetti and his wingman made another slow orbit. Even while the last elements were attacking, smoke began rising from several cars. The train was now stopped dead; its crew had either run away or been killed.

Righetti was almost out of ammunition, along with the other eleven pilots who had shot up the train. There was no point in hanging around; the only thing to do now was go home. Colonel Righetti radioed the squadron and ordered everyone to rendezvous at 15,000 feet. At the rendezvous point, he released the four 'top cover' Mustangs to find their own targets; he took the rest back to England.

As soon as he got back to Wormingford, Essex, the Colonel would give his squadron's intelligence officer a full run-down of the incident. To Righetti, the train looked a total wreck. It should take the enemy several days to move the junk off the tracks and clear the line again.

Between 15th October and 25th November more than 10,000 sorties were flown against railways and road transportation by the US Army Air Force and Fighter Command (which had changed its name back from Air Defence Great Britain on 15th October). Two trains just from the Central Works factory were caught by Allied fighters at the end of November, and given a thorough going over. The two trains carried forty A-4 missiles between them – all forty rockets had to be shipped back to Germany as scrap.

The results of these strafing attacks were sometimes spectacular. Back in August, Mustangs from the US 4th Fighter Group ran across a camouflaged freight train in a French rail yard. The fighters made three beam attacks; on the fourth pass, the train disintegrated in a fantastic explosion. Three of the Mustangs down 'on the deck' were blown about like dry leaves; the pilots flying 'top cover' called out that they had been hit by anti-aircraft fire. The fighter that caused the explosion vanished in the blast.

Haystacks caught fire on nearby farms, and roofs were blown off houses. A German troop train in the same yard was partly destroyed, with a heavy loss of life on board. There was nothing left of the freight cars that blew up except a string of craters, each was ten feet deep and thirty feet wide. Their cargo had been warheads for either Flying Bombs or V-2 rockets.

After the failure of Operation Market-Garden, air strikes were the only way of stopping – or at least slowing down – the rocket attack. But even though the Dutch road and rail system was constantly being harassed by American and British fighters, missile launchings kept increasing. During the first week of November, 12 V-2s hit London; during the second week, 15 V-2s arrived; during the third week, there were 27 V-2 incidents.

'This has been a week of bangs again,' one woman wryly commented. There still was no official word on what caused the bangs, but that didn't stop people from talking about them. Rumours were always more interesting than news reports, anyway.

'There are always two explosions, it seems,' Mrs Gwladys Cox relates what she had heard about the rockets. 'The things travel through the stratosphere in two parts. One, the container, explodes on reaching our atmosphere ... This releases the bomb itself, which drops, digging a deep crater and pulverising everything in its way.'

On 8th November the official silence was finally broken. At 6.35, a broadcast by the German news agency announced that the attack on London 'had been intensified during the last few weeks by another, and far more effective, weapon: the V-2'.

The radio announcement came two months after the first rocket hit London. Dr Josef Goebbels' Propaganda Ministry waited until the V-2 was a sure thing – the number of failed launches and the possibility of an Allied offensive had caused some serious doubts. But now the propaganda experts made up for lost time.

Britain's silence was claimed as evidence of the rocket's impact. 'Nothing speaks more eloquently of its devastating effect than the silence on the other side of the Channel.' The V-2s have 'literally taken London's breath away.'

'The train disintegrated in a fantastic explosion ...' Gun-camera stills, from a P-51 Mustang with the US 359th Fighter Group, show what happened to an ammunition train that was caught by a fighter sweep. The explosion destroyed the small white building in the foreground, and burned the paint off the bottom of the attacking Mustang. Strafing freight trains and road convoys was the only sure method of stopping the flow of launching supplies to the rocket sites.

Although the announcement was meant to bolster German morale, it was heard in London, also. Mrs Gwladys Cox commented, 'At last, the Germans are broadcasting news of their V-2 attacks.' Now that the word was out, the Churchill government *had* to make some sort of statement on the rockets.

On the day after the German announcement, Winston Churchill addressed the House of Commons. He confirmed the fact that long range missiles were being fired at Britain, but most of the speech was a mix of deception and propaganda. Churchill began by disclosing that 'long-range rockets ... have landed at widely scattered points in this country,' and predicted that the launching sites 'will doubtless be overrun by our forces in due course.'

Even after Churchill's statement, newspapers seemed reluctant to print anything about the missiles. News of the rockets appeared in American papers a day before the London press. On 10th November the headline of the New York *Sun* read, CHURCHILL ADMITS V-2 ROCKET HAS HIT BRITAIN, pushing aside the story of Franklin D. Roosevelt's re-election as President. It wasn't until the 11th that London's *Daily Express* proclaimed: V2: THE FULL STORY.

Now, the leading topic in everybody's mind was whether the rocket or the Flying Bomb was worse – just as people had compared the doodlebugs with the 1940-41 Blitz in July and August. There were some who felt that the Flying Bombs were more frightening. The buzzing throb of the pulse-jet and the sudden cutting out were as dreaded as the final explosion, while the rocket arrived before anybody knew it.

Because they arrived without warning, the V-2s could even be looked at with a sort of resigned detachment. There's nothing you can do to stop them anyway, so why worry? And because they travelled faster than sound, the story went that 'you'll never know about the one that gets you.' As US Navy Yeoman Don Cumming put it, 'If you heard it, the rocket hadn't hit you; if it hit you, you hadn't heard it.'

But for most, the abruptness of the V-2s arrival was its most terrifying feature. When a doodlebug cut out, there was always a few seconds to dive for cover, at least. With the rockets, there was no time to do anything. 'When we understood the V-2s travelled faster than sound, it was a different ballgame,' was one reaction.

'Without question, the V-2s were worse,' declared William H. Johnson of north London. 'The bang of the explosion was followed by the roar of the rocket's faster-than-sound descent,' he recalls, 'which ... made it seem bigger and more frightening.'

After the blast, 'black smoke rose up and drifted in the light wind until it stretched halfway across the horizon.' At night, Johnson would lie in bed and stare up at the ceiling, 'wondering if a rocket were already on the way down.'

In a letter, a girl left this impression of a V-2's totally unexpected impact: 'We were sitting at a lecture today at 4.10 p.m. when suddenly everything went black and the air was filled with glass and dust.'

This startling abruptness caused more than anxiety, however. Since no one had time to take shelter, the number killed and injured by the missiles was predictably high. Each time one of the sudden explosions jolted everyone for miles around, an average of four people died, double the death rate of the Flying Bombs.

When the first few missiles landed in September, they had been little more than a nuisance. But in November, several were hitting every day: on 12th November, there were four V-2 incidents; on the 13th, four more; on the 14th, another two incidents. By 20th November about 210 rockets reached England, with 95 hitting London. Four hundred and fifty six people had been killed in London alone, with hundreds more injured.

Besides causing actual physical damage, the rockets also had a psychological impact. If the pilotless Flying Bombs were sinister, the V-2s were almost supernaturally frightening – Mrs Gwladys Cox called them 'an affliction'. They also reinforeced Hitler's 'bogey-man' image – no matter how often Germany was bombed, they could always come up with a new and nasty surprise just when everybody thought the war was finally over.

Even though the V-2 was generally more feared, it disrupted daily life less than the Flying Bomb; because there was no air raid warning, people were not constantly running to shelter. Besides, basements or shelters were no longer a safe refuge; a plunging rocket could slam right through all but the deepest shelters. It didn't matter if a person was on the roof of a building or in the cellar if a rocket scored a direct hit – the results were the same.

A woman in a north London district, looking idly out her kitchen window, saw the building behind her flat disappear in an instant, with one tremendous *booom*. A V-2 had crashed through the roof and its one-ton warhead detonated inside the large brick structure. 'It went straight up in the air,' she remembers, 'and came down again in a pile of rubble.' There was nothing left of the place but a hole in the ground filled with bricks, splinters, and dirt. She was so astonished by the sight that she didn't even feel the long cut across her face, caused when her kitchen windows blew in.

Impacting at supersonic speeds, a rocket ploughed into the ground with such force that it buried itself in several feet of earth before exploding, even though its sensitive fuse was set to trigger the warhead immediately on contact.

Shock waves from a rocket explosion were not flat and concentric like a Flying Bomb's. If they had been visible, they would have resembled a funnel. The warhead's explosion opened up a crater about thirty feet wide. Blast waves shot out of the crater with murderous force, expanding as they moved up and out.

Everything within a radius of a quarter mile or more was reduced to an unstable hulk, the combined effect of the four-ton missile, empty of fuel, hitting at supersonic speeds, along with the one-ton warhead's concussion. An entire block of houses might be shattered, the roofs or whole outside walls blown away. A nineteen year-old member of the Woman's Auxiliary Air Force gives an idea of the aftermath of a rocket's arrival: 'Gaping holes in terraces, dresses still on hangers fluttering in what were once bedrooms, a saucepan still simmering on a suddenly cold stove ...'

November 25th 1944 was a Saturday. People all over London were doing their shopping; in the West End, a sprinkling of American uniforms could still be seen among the swarm. The New Cross Shopping Centre in the East London district of Deptford was as crowded as it always was on Saturday; in Woolworth's, shoppers practically walked on top of each other to choose from the limited selection on the shelves.

At 12.10 p.m. the Woolworth's building was shaken apart by a massive explosion. An instant later, the entire building collapsed into the basement. Everyone inside was thrown down into the cellar along with tons of beams and plaster; many were buried under the huge pile of debris.

A woman who survived the incident recalls, 'When I came to my senses ... my first impression was that there had been an earthquake.' She remembered 'a terrific crack, as though all the thunder I'd ever heard in my life had been gathered into one terrible roar. Then everything all around us collapsed.'

Afterward, everything seemed 'strangely quiet – suspended, as if everything had suddenly just stopped'. She had not been injured except for a few scratches, but was taken to hospital and treated for shock.

Not many were as lucky. One hundred and sixty-eight people had died. Some were killed outright by the rocket's impact and explosion; others were crushed or suffocated when the building caved in. Seventy to eighty bodies were dug out of Woolworth's alone. Eleven were never found.

If the rockets were not enough of an ordeal, the Flying Bombs were now making another appearance. Since mid-September, the bombs had been fired at London by a new and altogether different method. After the Pas de Calais ramps were captured by the Allied armies, the Luftwaffe began launching the pilotless planes in mid-air from Heinkel He111 bombers.

The twin-engine Heinkels, attached to *Kampfgeschwader* (bomb group) 53, operated from airfields in north-western Germany. *Kampfgeschwader* 53 had flown bombing missions against London in 1940 and 1941; now it was just a makeshift outfit, thrown together from odds and ends of other groups.

To escape radar detection, the He111s flew toward the English coast at extreme low altitudes; the Flying Bomb was slung under the Heinkel's port wing, inboard of the engine. The pilot climbed to 20,000 feet when the bomber neared its launching position, and would instruct the crew to start the Flying Bomb's engine and gyroscope. When everything was ready, the bomb was cast off.

As soon as it was released, the pilotless plane dropped sharply for several hundred feet. Some never pulled out, crashing into the North Sea with a huge fountain of spray. But most of the machines levelled off and continued along their pre-set course toward the eastern coastline of England.

This operation was not nearly as elaborate as the Flying Bomb offensive of the summer just past. An average of only one or two bombs a day was hitting London; some shots were aimed at the port of Southampton. These bombs were having a very limited effect on London, but were putting an added strain on the defences; the aerial shots were coming in from east instead of the Channel coast, going 'behind' the anti-aircraft belt and balloon barrage.

The new doodlebugs were also putting an added strain on London's already taut nerves. Every time the air raid sirens announced the approach of a buzz bomb, even the bravest souls developed a slight case of the flutters.

'Just to make things sound ordinary and friendly,' a woman wrote in her diary, 'we have a siren once or twice a night with a doodle or two – we couldn't do without those, of course!' But the humour turned sour as she continued.

> How lucky are the people who are away from London! I get letters telling me they long to be back but my God, how pleasant it must be to live without this persistently dropping-wearying banging and shuddering.

Unteroffizier Otto Neuchel was as depressed and embittered as anyone in London. Neuchel knew that there was always a chance that he might get wounded; he hoped that he might even get a medal or maybe a promotion out of it. But he never expected to end up this way.

While his Flying Bomb unit was moving through Holland, all vehicles came to a stop to let some local horse-drawn vehicles plod across the road. Neuchel got down off his transport to stretch his legs. He hadn't gone very far when he found himself wedged in between another transport and a passing farm wagon. Before he could get out of the way, the wagon's heavy wooden cart wheel ran over his right foot.

Now, Neuchel was in a field hospital near the Dutch-German border, his crushed right foot in a heavy cast. He couldn't move more than a few feet at a time, hopping along on his left leg. His unit had just pulled out without him – Neuchel was told bluntly that there was no room in the launch crew for an injured man,

'... the Flying Bomb was slung under the Heinkel's port wing, inboard of the engine.' A Flying Bomb in position for an air launch, mounted under the wing of a Heinkel He 111 bomber.

'... a hole in the ground filled with bricks, splinters, and dirt.' All that remains of a row of houses in south-east London after a direct hit by a V-2 rocket.

especially someone who was stupid enough to get himself run over by a horse cart, and he would have to stay behind.

To make matters worse, Neuchel found out that his old antagonist General Shithead had just been promoted. There just wasn't any justice at all.

During November, the number of missiles launched at Britain increased dramatically. But besides quantity, accuracy had also taken a step forward. Eighty-two rockets landed on London – an increase of fifty from the month of October.

The sudden improvement was largely because the launching crews were now getting a better grade of missile. Under a new system called *warme Semmel*, or 'hot cakes', rockets no longer sat about for weeks before launching.

As soon as a new A-4 missile left the Central Works plant, it was moved by train to an assembly and test site near the Dutch coast. At the 'field store', electrical tests and minor repairs were carried out, and the rocket's warhead was attached. All tests completed, the missile was turned over to the launching batteries. Within three or four days after leaving its factories, before delicate systems had a chance to corrode, the missile thundered off into the stratosphere.

Since 9th November Walchern Island was no longer occupied by the Wehrmacht. After a sharp nine-day battle, the German commander surrendered Walchern Island and 10,000 troops to British and Canadian forces. The way to the port of Antwerp was now clear; all fifty-four miles of the port's seaward approaches were controlled by Allied forces. But the rocket launchings went on, from The Hague and its outskirts.

Even though the missiles were now fresh from the Central Works factory, launching mishaps continued. Dutch intelligence put the failure fate for launchings at 8%, but Hans van Wouw Koeleman thinks it was more like 20% to 25%. Some rockets blew up on their launch stands, killing and injuring crew members. Some failed to ignite at all. Others hung in the air for a moment, then crashed to earth and blew up or fell into the sea.

The first few accidents showed Hans van Wouw Koeleman and his family how devastating a failed V-2 could be. Whenever they heard the roar of a rocket blast-off, everyone would begin to count the seconds. After thirty seconds, they were safe; if the engine stopped after thirty seconds or more had gone by, the rocket would either crash into the North Sea or fall on the other side of the city.

When the engine cut out before the thirty second limit, that was the worst time. The missile would slow down and 'literally hang in the air for a few seconds' before it began to fall. Young Hans saw one rocket skip through a meadow, its engine kicking off and on, with a German specialist chasing it on a motor bike. It finally blew up on the ground.

Most of the 'fizzles' exploded on impact; if the warhead did not go off, German specialists would try to defuse it. Many of the failed shots fell on The Hague. The detonation of the 2,000lb warhead, along with the alcohol and liquid oxygen supply, blew up hundreds of houses and caused thousands of civilian casualties.

That old 'air burst' problem had never been completely solved, either. Rockets frequently ruptured in the upper atmosphere, high above the North Sea. On 12th November a missile blew up in mid-air over London's Victoria Station. Astonished passers-by saw a puff of smoke blossom in the sky as if by magic, followed a few seconds later by a distant explosion and a hail of metal fragments.

Although the launching batteries in and around The Hague hit London eighty-two times in November, the crews of 444 Battery and 485 Detachment had no real idea where their missiles were landing. They could only set their gyro mechanisms and hope for the best.

The intelligence problem had not improved since the Flying Bomb phase. Neutral journalists still refused to co-operate with German agents, and the agents themselves could not always get their information through to Germany.

When messages did get through, they were not always accurate or received clearly. At the beginning of November, Berlin got word that Euston Railway Station had been destroyed. Not only was this a false report – Euston Station had not been touched – but somehow 'Euston' became garbled into 'Epsom'.

The lack of reliable information did not stop the Propaganda Ministry from boasting about their latest Vengeance Weapon. 'The explosions not only smashed whole rows of houses,' declared a radio broadcast, 'they pulverised everything – tiles, bricks, stones, and especially glass were literally pulverised after an explosion.'

Not everyone was convinced, however. A number of Adolf Hitler's advisors – including Reichsminister Albert Speer, after some thought about the matter – believed the A-4 project was too much of a drain on the Third Reich's economy. Speer could see that rocket production was diverting manpower and resources away from vital anti-aircraft programmes.

Throughout October and November, British and American bombers bomber forces continued to roam at will over Germany, crippling German industry. The US Eighth Air Force alone mounted sorties of 1,000 bombers or more, which dropped thousands of tons of high explosives on each raid. Albert Speer and many senior Luftwaffe officers argued in favour of building up anti-aircraft defences by promoting projects like the *Wasserfall* anti-aircraft missile and the Me262 jet fighter.

The *Wasserfall* was a 25 foot-long liquid-fuelled ground-to-air missile. It carried a 100-lb warhead and had an effective altitude of 50,000 feet. But the *Wasserfall* project had been cancelled; all *Wasserfall* engineers were re-assigned to the A-4 project.

Even more effective was the Messerschmitt Me262 jet-propelled interceptor. Travelling at speeds over 400 mph, the Me262 had no trouble penetrating the fighter screen that protected the American bombers. The new German jet could easily outmanoeuvre even the newest P-51 Mustangs.

In October 1944 the first jet-equipped unit, *Jagdgeschwader* (fighter squadron) 7, had been formed and equipped with the Me262. Even though only three or four of the fighters could be sent up every day, the jet-propelled Messerschmitts shot down 22 Allied aircraft by the end of the month. The jets were claiming better than ten enemy planes for each one of their own losses.

But Adolf Hitler wanted nothing to do with defence. Even though the Me262 jet fighter had proved its worth, Hitler would not even allow the plane to be called a 'fighter'. He wanted it loaded down with bombs to attack London, striking back in retaliation for the raids on Berlin and other cities.

Hitler was still convinced that he could bring back his 1940 victories by attacking London. Only the V-2 rocket could bring the war to Britain; the Luftwaffe did not have the fuel to launch anything resembling a new 'Blitz', even if the bombers could manage to get through the Allied fighter screen. The long-range guided missile was the last offensive weapon he had left. Adolf Hitler had no intention of cancelling the rocket project, regardless of what his advisors told him.

CHAPTER ELEVEN

'God Damn – Here We Go Again'

Even though British, American, and Canadian armoured and infantry divisions were at the borders of the Third Reich, German civilians were still being treated to quite a few cheerful news reports every day.

During the first week of December 1944, the Propaganda Ministry announced that the Wehrmacht was holding its own all along the Western Front in a 'brilliant defensive battle'. Attention was focused mainly upon the town of Colmar, about ten miles west of the Rhine in central Germany. The garrison at Colmar had dug itself in, and kept beating back all attacks. Josef Goebbels proudly insisted that 'the German soldier is making the enemy pay for every foot of ground'.

But the main item in Dr Goebbels' news releases was the V-2 rocket. At every opportunity, the revenge motive was mentioned – the *V-Waffen* were striking back in retaliation for the enemy air attacks against German cities. And best of all, the missiles were unstoppable, the reports went on; they could not be detected in any way or shot down.

In June civilians had been enthusiastic about the V-1 Flying Bomb and asked, 'When will V-2 be due?' But the Flying Bombs failed to tilt events in Germany's favour, which led to disillusion. When the V-2 became operational, spirits rose again – maybe this one would do it!

These news broadcasts had some effect upon civilian morale, but nothing decisive or long lasting. It soon became clear that the rockets were not going to win the war, nor would they keep American and British bombers from making their devastating attacks.

Nearly every day, the powerful Allied air fleets continued to blast German cities at will. On the last day of November 1,200 heavy bombers flew over Germany, encountering only light and sporadic opposition. Eleven days later 1,467 bombers attacked targets throughout the Third Reich; resistance once again was minimal.

'Life in the bombed towns and industrial districts grows worse every week,' the Swedish newspaper *Stockholm-Tidningen* reported about bomb-ruined Western Germany.

> There is no water, gas, or light – everything has been destroyed by bombing ... Only the bare essentials of public life can be maintained. It is clearly realised in Germany that things will become even worse.

Although some people continued to believe, a growing number stopped paying attention to the V-2 reports. If the rockets were as terrible as the newspapers said, how could the enemy keep sending so many bombers over?

In December 1944 Britain's Air Ministry decided that bombing liquid oxygen factories might succeed where other attempts to stop the long-range missiles had failed. Experts drew up a list of eighteen factories that manufactured liquid oxygen – ten were inside Germany, eight were in Holland.

But the eight plants in Holland, considered to be the most important, had been built in residential areas. Attacking these factories would require pinpoint accuracy; even the slightest bombing error might result in hundreds of civilian deaths. Because of an agreement with The Hague government regarding such targets in built-up districts, not one of the liquid oxygen factories in Holland was bombed. Only two of the German plants were attacked; this had no effect upon the supply of liquid oxygen to the rocket launching crews.

Fighter Command and the US Ninth Air Force also stepped up their 'armed reconnaissance' flights over The Hague. Hundreds of sorties were flown during late November-early December. Sometimes contacts from the Dutch underground tipped off the always close-by fighter-bombers.

Members of the Dutch resistance very quickly learned that the arrival of a rocket-carrying *Meillerwagen* trailer in their area, along with the rest of the rocket battery's vehicles, was the sure sign of an impending launch. Hans van Wouw Koeleman knew that the underground was in touch, 'because the Spitfires and Typhoons were never long in coming to shoot the Germans to bits' after a missile shot.

All along the *Rijks Straatweg*, the road north from The Hague through Wassenaar, foxholes had been dug for quick shelter in case of air attack. Whenever the planes came, Hans van Wouw Koeleman and his fellows would dive into the holes, along with any German soldiers in the vicinity. At one place along the Hague-Wassenaar road, a large sign informed passers-by, *Achtung, Tiefflieger-angriffe: Deckungslöcher Links* – 'Caution, Strafing Attacks: foxholes on left.'

But the rocket launching crews were as aware of the underground's moves as the underground was of theirs. They realised that the launch vehicles were a dead giveaway; by December, each firing unit included a camouflage platoon. Field training now emphasised camouflage, for concealing the tankers and trailers from the air. Vehicles that had to remain in the launch area were dug in and covered with concealment netting; the rest were dispersed and hidden in the woods.

Although the missiles flew too high and fast to be intercepted, there are at least two instances where a V-2 was shot at immediately after leaving its firing platform, when it was still relatively slow-moving. During a sweep over Holland, the pilot of a Spitfire saw a missile rising in the distance and decided to give chase. He pushed the throttle as far forward as it would go and fired his cannon at the fast-climbing target, but it was out of range within seconds and no hits were scored.

In a second mid-air attack, the missile was actually shot down. A squadron of four-engine B-24 Liberators of the US 34th Bomb Group was returning to England, flying over the Low Countries at about 10,000 feet, when a V-2 passed right through their formation. To an engineer-gunner aboard one of the bombers, the rocket looked like 'a telephone pole with fire squirting out of its tail'.

Right after he spotted it, the gunner heard a machine gun open fire at the missile – 'a left waist gunner in our squadron let fly a burst and down it went'. Because of the incredible delicacy of a V-

2's workings, even a single .50 calibre machine gun bullet could puncture a fuel tank or hit a line and send the rocket crashing to earth. After the B-24 got back to base, its crew chief painted a V-2 on the side of the plane.

In spite of the many attempts to stop the launchings, only rocket malfunctions and an occasional freak shot kept the missiles from coming down in Britain. An average of four or five V-2s hit London every day during the early part of December, with as many hitting the neighbouring county of Essex, just to the east.

At the beginning of December a rocket exploded in the River Thames, not far from the Savoy Hotel. It sent a huge geyser of muddy water high into the air, and blew out windows all up and down the river – the Savoy Hotel lost all of its windows again, for the seventh time since 1940. Later in the day, people gathered on Waterloo Bridge and the Embankment to stare at the spot where the missile landed.

During the same time in December, Margaret Hutcheson – the US Red Cross girl who had mistaken the air raid sirens for the noon whistle last June – was back in London for a few days' leave. She was staying at the Savoy Hotel, in a room on the top floor facing the river – the hotel management still was having no trouble renting the south-facing rooms to Americans.

Miss Hutcheson could hear an occasional air-launched Flying Bomb trundle overhead while she was lying in bed at night. The pulse-jet engine's rattling noise kept her awake, and each time one of the bombs cut out she would listen and count the seconds until the explosion.

While she had been on duty near the south coast, Miss Hutcheson had been able to hear the anti-aircraft guns firing at the bombs during the night, but it all seemed far away to her. Now she was right in the middle of the Vengeance Weapons attack and, for the first time, was really afraid and 'thouroughly hated the Germans'.

Air launched Flying Bombs were still hitting London, but only at an average rate of one or two per day – a total failure from the Luftwaffe's point of view. About 650 of the pilotless aircraft had been launched since early September, but only 50-odd ever got as far as London.

Many crashed into the North Sea just after release from its Heinkel He111 mother ship; others went astray and landed in vacant fields or splashed into the Channel. Thirteen of the Heinkel bombers were shot down by RAF fighters, putting a real strain on *Kampfgeschwader* 53's already limited resources.

The major worry in London was the V-2 rockets, which continued to run up an impressive number of killed and injured. Fear was more widespread over the rockets than it had ever been with the Flying Bombs.

During the summer just past, the pilotless planes had been the butt of many a grim joke and were tagged with a wide range of cute-vulgar nicknames. Nearly everyone had at least one 'doodlebug story', just as there had been many amusing bomb stories during the Blitz. But the missiles inspired no names or catchphrases. People rarely discussed them at all, hating and fearing them too much to talk about them.

In their room on Blandford Street in London's West End, US Navy Yeoman Don Cumming and his roommate were playing cards on the night of Wednesday, 6th December 1944. At about 10 p.m. the lights suddenly went dim; an instant later, the two of them heard a very loud explosion. At first they thought the blast must have been several miles away, but, after thinking about the brief time span between the dimmed lights and the bang, decided that it must have been somewhere in their neighbourhood. They went out to see exactly where the rocket had landed.

A half-mile away, Technical Sergeant Dick Dudley was broadcasting an American Forces programme from the BBC studios in Portland Place. He was actually just signing off for the night, playing phonograph records of 'God Save the King' and 'The Star-Spangled Banner', when the rocket hit. Even though the studio was completely walled off, having no windows at all, the explosion had enough force to knock the needle right off the record.

Nearly a mile away from the rocket's point of impact, at the Rainbow Club in Piccadilly, the chandeliers swayed from the concussion. American airman Truman Smith felt the shock but had no idea what had happened – he had seen quite a few buzz bombs on previous trips into London, but this was his first V-2. Smith was sitting on the ground floor of the US Servicemen's club, reading a *Buck Rogers in the 25th Century* comic book, and wondered, 'What the hell was that?'

The rocket had slammed into Duke Street, next to Selfridges Department Store. A passing taxi was blown into Selfridges' window by the blast – the driver and passengers were never found. Several American soldiers, probably also passers-by, were killed outright by the explosion.

Yeoman Don Cumming and his roommate only had to walk about 400 yards to reach the scene. They found the restaurant where they had eaten only a few hours before completely demolished; sprawled on the pavement outside were the bodies of several GIs.

The Rescue Squad arrived within a few minutes after the blast, and began digging through the rubble in search of other bodies. A crowd very quickly gathered to watch the rescue men; the audience included a dazed American soldier, his uniform dirty and torn and his ragged trousers actually smouldering. This was the section of the city that Londoners called the 'American Occupied Zone'; one unmistakably American voice called out to his battered fellow GI, 'Hey, Charlie, your ass is on fire.'

A trail of broken glass went right round the block. Most of the windows in Selfridges Department Store were knocked out, along with all the windows for quite a distance along Oxford Street. Mixed with the slivers of glass were glittering bits of red and green – the ornaments from all the Christmas displays had been blown out into the street with the display windows.

Sometimes a single event will blow up all out of proportion and trigger an exaggerated public response, causing people to direct all their pent-up anger at persons who had nothing to do with the incident. The Selfridges V-2 explosion was just such an occurrence. Destroying Christmas ornaments might seem a small matter, but during this sixth Christmas at war it made a lot of people very angry. London's anger was not directed at the Germans so much as at Winston Churchill and his War Cabinet.

Duncan Sandys' announcement that 'The Battle of London is over' still raised hackles every time people thought about it, even three months afterward. Since Sandys' announcement, the war had intensified. Some said that things were at their worst since 1941. The loud, startling booms happened several times a day, and there was no way to stop them; having one of the rockets blow up Christmas displays on Oxford Street was adding insult to injury.

This feeling of discontent was not confined to the public. A Member of Parliament, as anxious about the war as anyone, complained that Winston Churchill 'won't tell us when we are going to win the war until at least 24 hours after the German army ... has laid down its arms'.

American Intelligence worker Richard Baker was even more pessimistic. Despite all evidence that Germany would be forced to give up the fight by early summer in 1945, Baker was no longer absolutely sure that the Allies would win the war. In June 1940 Baker pointed out, most Germans believed that Hitler would be in London by autumn.

Richard Baker would not have to worry about many more V-2 attacks, however. Within the month, Baker and his Intelligence unit would be transferred to Paris.

Listeners to the nine o'clock news on 16th December 1944 heard that German troops had broken through the American lines in Belgium earlier that day. Information on the strength of the attack was sketchy, but the report had an ominous ring to it.

There was good reason for concern. At 5.30 that morning, 24 German divisions – 250,000 infantrymen and 1,000 tanks – had thrown their full weight against the lightly defended Ardennes front in Belgium. Six American divisions held this sector – known as the 'Ghost Front' because of its peace and quiet, despite being within rifle range of the Siegfried Line pillboxes – but three of the divisions were green, just over from the States, and three were exhausted from six months of combat. The Wehrmacht and Panzer divisions ploughed right through these troops along a 50-mile front, and kept pouring through the lines all day long.

During the next few days, news from the Continent kept getting worse. 'RUNDSTEDT LAUNCHES FULL-SCALE ATTACK' was the *Daily Telegraph*'s headline on 18th December. The US Army Air Force and RAF had been grounded by fog and bad weather; protected from air attacks by bad weather, the German forces continued to roll into Belgium.

By the 19th, German armour and infantry had advanced more than 40 miles inside US lines, overwhelming any American units that tried to stop them. 'The Battle of The Bulge', as some were already calling it, was beginning to look like a major victory for the German army.

Psychologically, the attack could not have been better timed. Nobody, not even General Eisenhower and certainly not anybody in London, expected a new offensive. The public believed that Germany was being worn down, and that it was only a matter of weeks before the fighting ended. But now, the war suddenly seemed very far away again.

The most immediate reaction was stunned surprise. 'How could they stage an offensive?' wondered a girl in north London. 'Where did they get all the supplies, all the equipment ...?' Technical Sergeant Dick Dudley didn't know what to think. 'We thought the war really was all over by then,' he remembers.

A remark by an American army private, recovering from combat wounds in a hospital near London, summed up the feeling of just about everyone in the Allied camp. The soldier had hoped that the fighting would be over before he was due to rejoin his unit across the Channel, but von Rundstedt's offensive killed that thought. In his diary, he wrote just one short, frustrated sentence: 'God damn – here we go again.'

Although the drive was aimed at recapturing the port of Antwerp, nobody realised it at the time. Once again, the rumour mills started up. Some people said that the German army was pushing toward Calais and then right across the Channel to England. Another, more believable, rumour insisted that the Wehrmacht was heading for Paris.

The German offensive had one benefit for London – the V-2 attack had slackened to only about one rocket per day. To soften up Antwerp, both the rockets and Flying Bombs were aimed at the Belgian port instead of the British capital.

Colonel Max Wachtel's *Flakregiment* 155(W), minus Unteroffizier Otto Neuchel, who was still in a hospital in Holland, began launching their Flying Bombs at Antwerp in mid-December. The new ramps were in central Holland, only about 110 miles from

Antwerp. At that range, the pilotless planes were much more accurate than they had been against London; the machines destroyed a good part of the city.

Not every shot hit its mark, however. One German infantryman was nearly hit by a Flying Bomb that strayed off course. His unit was just outside Malmedy, Belgium when a buzz bomb fell short and exploded on an empty barn about 250 yards away. He wasn't hurt but 'there was a psychological effect,' he explained. 'I needed new underpants in a hurry.'

Even more intense than the Flying Bombs was the rocket attack. Twenty-six of the missiles hit Antwerp on a single day, 23rd December. Three days later, 26 more of the missiles came down on the port city. On the 16th, a V-2 scored a direct hit on the crowded Rex cinema, killing 271 people.

Julian Roffman, attached to the 4th Canadian Armoured Division, had been ordered to film the unloading of supplies from merchant ships at Antwerp's docks. Roffman and the other members of his detachment arrived in Antwerp just after a V-2 had blown apart an open market. He saw a crater, 'very deep and wide,' where the market had been, along with 'bits and pieces of people and produce and livestock and buildings all mixed together.'

Roffman and the other soldiers got out of their vehicle to see if they could help. But the men had no equipment for taking care of that many wounded, and were pushed out of the way by ambulances and rescue vehicles. After that, the film crew decided not to go on to their destination. Everybody got back aboard their vehicle, turned around and began their return trip to Brussels. All the way back, no one spoke; the men stared silently ahead and smoked one cigarette after another.

Antwerp's misfortune turned out to be London's gain, however. The rocket let-up allowed Londoners to prepare for Christmas without the risk of being killed by a V-2, at least.

Christmas 1944 was not a very cheerful one. The food ration was better than last year, however; everyone was allowed extra sugar and margarine for Christmas week, and there were some turkeys in the shop windows. But everything else was scarce, shoddy, and very expensive. Children's toys cost 'outrageous sums of money', according to one woman, and were not worth buying.

Mostly, though, it was just that nobody felt much like a holiday mood. People were depressed and worried about the German offensive, and were especially uneasy about the sudden rocket lull. During the Blitz, London learned that a quiet time usually meant that the worst was to come afterward. Most of the heavy raids of 1940 and 1941 came after long periods, sometimes as long as several weeks, without an alert.

'I think this past week has been one of the most trying weeks of the war,' Gwladys Cox commented on 23rd December.

> Very bad weather; all the business of Christmas; trying to keep cheerful in spite of the grave news about the success of the German putsch on the Western Front. So many people had hoped the war would be over by Christmas, and here we are ...

Christmas Day itself was overcast, just as the weather had been for the past ten days. The temperature was below freezing, blanketing parks and squares with a crisp sheet of hoar frost while the sun, crimson and high, did its best to penetrate the mist.

There were no alerts and no rockets to interrupt the subdued festivities. Gwladys Cox noted that the day was 'entirely peaceful'. Her only complaint was about the Christmas chicken, which was 'almost too tough to eat'. Also, the Underground trains were not running; the train men went on strike over not getting two days holiday for Christmas.

On the day after Christmas the German offensive reached its limit. American armour and infantry were now fighting the German drive to a standstill, fifty-five miles inside Belgium. The fog and low cloud had lifted over the Continent; the US Army Air Force and RAF were back, harassing the enemy with bombing and strafing attacks and air lifting supplies to American troops.

The tanks of the US 2nd Armoured Division stopped the Panzer spearhead dead in its tracks on the 27th. From then on, the mighty German armies would slowly retreat until they were back behind the Siegfried Line defences.

But even though the Wehrmacht was withdrawing, the surprise of the attack still had everyone off balance. Rumours were still plentiful – they no longer involved the German armies as much as the secret weapons. If the German High Command could pull off such an offensive, they could do anything. 'That man Hitler, you can't put anything past him,' went the popular saying.

Just before the Battle of the Bulge began, 'reliable' agents in Turkey and Argentina reported that German missiles would begin hitting cities on the east coast of the United States within thirty days. (Plans for a two-stage 'New York rocket', called *A-10*, had been drawn up. But the *A-10* never got beyond the blueprint stage.)

Also, there was talk of launching Flying Bombs from U-Boats; the bombs would be launched at American cities near the Atlantic coast, notably New York. Gossip-mongers also mentioned a 'V3', 'V-4', and a 'final weapon'. One source reported that the 'final weapon' was the atomic bomb, which would be mounted on a V-2 rocket. A second rumour agreed that the 'final weapon' was an atom bomb, but claimed that it would be used with a two-stage missile and fired at America.

Adolf Hitler was told by his leading military advisors that the Belgian offensive had failed. The River Meuse could not be crossed and Antwerp would not be re-taken. But Hitler still had no intention of giving up.

Hitler lived in a drug-induced dream-world where it would always be 1940. But he was still in command of all German armed forces. His mind was constantly occupied with two recurring themes: attack and revenge. And his prime target was the same as it had been in 1940 – London.

As New Year approached the weather in London became clear, although it remained cold. The battle news from Belgium was improving, although there were now more sudden booms than there had been lately.

From his home in The Hague, 14-year-old Hans van Wouw Koeleman still watched the rockets lifting off from their firing platforms. He managed to see quite a few launchings, and sometimes more than just his curiosity was rewarded.

Once, when a rocket crashed after launching, young Hans and his friends found a liquid oxygen tank, 'all covered with ice'. They put it in Hans' little firewood pushcart and brought it to the German sentry at the gate of the restricted zone.

The sentry detained Hans and the others until a Luftwaffe major arrived to take possession of the frost-covered tank. Everybody was very nice about the whole thing; the Germans even gave Hans a loaf of *Kommisbrot* – sour dough army bread – some butter, and a piece of cheese. Hans almost succeeded in stealing a Luger pistol that was lying on a chair, but had to give it back.

Now that the drive to Antwerp had failed, London once again became the main target for the rocket launching batteries. Hans van Wouw Koeleman remembers 'one memorable occasion' on New Year's Eve; just before midnight, at five and again at two minutes before twelve o'clock, two rockets were launched in quick succession – 'to wish Londoners a Happy New Year'.

Both shots fizzled. One of the missiles fell on a nearby army barracks, killing many German soldiers. When he heard about the incident, Hans' father cracked open one of his last bottles of Dutch gin and 'hoisted one', toasting the 'favourable results the Germans had achieved that night'.

During the rocket lull, some Londoners had been saying, 'Watch out – the worst is still to come.' Now, it was beginning to look as though they had been right.

The war looked like it was going to be over several times throughout the past year. Spirits had risen after D-Day, again after the July breakout from the Beachhead, and rose for a third time during the Arnhem airdrop. Shortly afterward, spirits had dropped again just as dramatically.

Now the Germans were retreating, but what would they be doing a month from now? The fighting was far from finished, and the rocket threat was still as alive as ever. The inevitable toast for New Year 1945 was, 'Well, here's to the last year of the war.' It was seldom offered with much conviction.

CHAPTER TWELVE

'The Last Bullet'

January 30th 1945 was the twelfth anniversary of Adolf Hitler's coming to power as Chancellor of Germany. But no ceremonies or celebrations marked the occasion. Munitions Minister Albert Speer had drawn up a memorandum to Hitler, which was delivered on the 30th; Speer began his report by flatly stating that the war was already lost.

Exactly one month to the day after the Panzer and Wehrmacht divisions rolled through the American front lines in Belgium, on 16th January 1945, all the German soldiers that would ever return were back behind the Siegfried Line – 120,000 men had been killed, wounded, or taken prisoner, losses that could not be replaced.

Four days earlier, on 12th January, the Russian armies had begun their own offensive on the Eastern Front. One hundred and eighty divisions began overrunning Poland and eastern Germany; one German general called the attack a 'Russian tidal wave'. The German army had spent its last reserves in the Battle of the Bulge, and had nothing that could stop this onslaught. By the end of January, the Russian forces had advanced 220 miles; they were well inside Germany, only 100 miles from Berlin.

When Adolf Hitler read Albert Speer's gloomy report of 30th January, he complained that Speer always had something 'unpleasant' to say to him. Hitler refused to see Speer alone afterwards – too depressing. There were still the *Wunderwaffen*, the 'miracle weapons', which Hitler insisted would drive the enemy back.

Hitler was confident that a fleet of new U-Boats, large, long-range electric boats, would soon begin preying on Allied shipping. The sea lanes between Britain and the United States would be cut, he thought, slowly starving the Allied armies. In the air, the jet-powered Messerschmitt Me 262 fighter was already bringing down an astounding number of American bombers. When the jet fighters became available to the Luftwaffe in large numbers, they would drive the enemy bomber fleets from the sky.

There were other weapons as well, Hitler insisted. The V-1 Flying Bomb and V-2 rocket were already hitting London in retaliation for the Allied air raids. Rocket production had been increased, in the coming weeks the attack would be stepped up. Also there was the atomic project. If an atomic bomb could be perfected, such a weapon would make the enemy give up the fight or face unprecedented destruction.

But, as usual, Adolf Hitler was living in a dream world. Most of the miracle machines he was counting on existed only in his own mind.

Those new electric U-Boats might have played havoc with Allied shipping had there been enough of them. But of 126 that were commissioned, only two U-Boats put to sea by mid-February. It was the same story with the jet fighters. They were far superior to anything the British or Americans could put in the air, but there were too few of them to stop the great bomber formations of the US Army Air Force and the RAF.

As for the atomic bomb project, it was put out of action by a combination of Allied bombers and infighting between Nazi officials and scientists. High-ranking SS men arrested a number of atomic technicians on charges of 'suspected disloyalty'.

Hitler could not face the fact that the war had already been lost, just as Albert Speer had said, and that it would be only a matter of time before the Third Reich was completely overrun. As long as he had any armed forces left at all, he would use them against the enemy. With the Luftwaffe grounded because of lack of fuel and his last remaining troops fighting a defensive battle, the V-2 rocket was Hitler's only hope of striking back. As long as he still had the long-range guided missiles, Hitler convinced himself that the war might be turned around in spite of everything.

More than ten times every day in January, the tall, gleaming missiles made their graceful ascent from launching platforms near

The Hague. In the cold winter air, the vapour trails formed a little sooner than usual. Even with the naked eye, an observer could follow the white, wavy contrail for quite a distance as the rockets curved into the stratosphere on their way to England.

During the month of January, 114 of the missiles ended their short, faster-than-sound journey by slamming into London at more than 5,000 miles per hour. It was the worst month for rockets so far: in November, 82 incidents had been reported and, because of the attack on Antwerp, in December there were only 47. Another 71 rockets came down on Essex, shots aimed at London that fell short.

Factories producing everything from munitions to civilian clothing were damaged or destroyed, along with warehouses stocked with food. Houses continued to take a beating; on impact a V-2 could shatter houses for several blocks. On 14th January twenty houses in south London were demolished by a single missile, and another fifty suffered serious damage. Three other rockets hit London on the 14th, as well as six air launched Flying Bombs – the last pilotless planes fired from the twin-engine Heinkel bombers.

Apart from killing and injuring, the blast from an exploding rocket was now causing another kind of casualty. January 1945 was the coldest month in living memory; the combination of freezing weather with blown-out windows and no roofs produced much discomfort – frostbite, head colds and influenza.

'It is a bitterly cold day, with driving snow showers – the worst sort of weather to be without windows,' Mrs Gwladys Cox commented early in January. Three weeks later, the weather was just as bad. 'Here, we are certainly frozen up,' said Mrs Cox, 'no kitchen fire; drinking water from a pail from the Tomlins next door.' Washing water came from a garden pool, which did not freeze.

Hilda Neal of South Kensington adds, 'It has been a bitterly cold week or two: snow, frost, ice, sleet, and winds from the Arctic.' To make matters worse, coal was in short supply; people gathered it up in buckets and wheelbarrows wherever they could find it.

Millions of windowpanes had been destroyed by the rocket explosions. All over London, ragged wooden or paper patches covered blasted windows; sometimes, there was no covering at all.

'Even with the naked eye, an observer could follow the white, wavy contrail for quite a distance ...' During a bombing mission over enemy territory, the navigator of a US Army Air Force B-24 Liberator took this photo of a V-2 rocket's vapour trail. Less than four minutes later, the rocket will slam into Greater London. The photograph illustrates the phenomenon that General Dornberger called 'Frozen Lightning'.

Glassmakers could not turn out panes fast enough, and glaziers had their hands full trying to repair all the windows. Thousands of man hours in war production factories were lost because of illness.

'For eight days, we had no front door.' In an article entitled 'London's Bombed Houses: A Defeat on the Home Front' from the magazine *Picture Post*, a young woman describes living in her blast-damaged home in south London.

> Mother and I went to bed with a trip-wire over the threshold. I fell over it myself four times. It was nine days before we had anything over our windows, eleven before we got a sheet over our roof.

As bad as things were in London, they were even worse in Germany. Shortages were becoming increasingly severe. 'Gasless hours' were introduced in many cities – the gas was cut off between 7 and 10 a.m. and again from 2 to 6 p.m. Transportation was getting worse all the time, and deliveries of all goods were less and less dependable. In one city, all the newspaper delivery women left town after a particularly bad air raid.

Neutral journalists wrote sombre reports on the war-weariness of German city dwellers. When civil authorities ordered trench digging in the streets for the defence of Berlin, according to the Swiss newspaper *Der Bund*, the directive was not only ignored but was laughed at.

And the bombing went on. Throughout January, huge formations of Allied planes struck at objectives across Germany – 'wide-spread targets', according to the official communiqués – usually numbering 1,000 or more bombers per sortie.

February brought no relief. On the 3rd, 1,000 B-17 Flying Fortresses bombed oil targets near the Saxon city of Magdeburg and rail yards in Berlin. On the following day, newspapers in Sweden were filled with grim stories about the air raid. As the month went on, other cities were added to the growing list: Nürnberg, Leipzig, Berlin again.

Eight hundred RAF Lancaster bombers attacked the city of Dresden on the night of 13th February, dropping tons of high explosives and 650,000 incendiaries. Within minutes after the first bombs fell, large fires had broken out in the centre of Dresden; the fires were clearly visible to the bomber crews flying over the city, marking the target for later attacks.

In the early morning hours of 14th February, 311 US Eighth Air Force B-17 Flying Fortresses dropped more high explosives on the still raging fires. By that time, much of Dresden had already been destroyed; the last bombs helped the fires to spread out still further. Many thousands of people died in the air raid and resulting fire-storm; one estimate claims as many as 135,000.

After the fires died down, someone painted a message on a charred pavement: 'Thank you, dear Führer.' The German newspaper *Das Schwarze Korps* declared, 'It cannot be worse than it is now.'

At the end of February, the Russian drive into eastern Germany forced the rocket technicians to evacuate Peenemünde. More than 4,000 staff members and whole train loads of equipment moved from Peeremünde to the Harz Mountains in Central Germany.

Another complex was to be built near the town of Bleicheröde, twelve miles from the Central Works plant at Nordhausen. Like the Central Works factory, this new site was to have been under-ground, 2,000 feet below the earth's surface. Some of the rocket men had a strong suspicion – correct, as it turned out – that the war would be over before the new testing facilities could be finished.

Meanwhile, the rocket launching batteries continued firing the long, pointed missiles from Holland. Allied fighter sweeps kept shooting up every freight train they saw, but supplies got through just the same. Liquid oxygen, alcohol, and necessary equipment – including the rockets themselves – were delivered to firing crews under cover of night. Launches would be prepared in the early morning hours, and the missiles were fired from mid-morning onward.

Julian Roffman, who had seen a V-2's effects on an open market in Antwerp, now had the chance to see the rockets from another point of view. His unit, a forward scouting section with the 4th Canadian Armoured Division, was moving north into Holland; Roffman's job was to take motion pictures of the advance. Near the town of Nijmegen, the drive was held up by heavy mortar fire. In between mortar barrages, Roffman was able to see V-2 rockets being launched in the distance.

'We would watch those vapour trails going straight up,' Roffman reported, 'and then disappear into the stratosphere.' He saw several launchings. '... we could see the thin, curling smoke trails of the launched V-2s as they were fired toward London or wherever they were aimed.'

Before each launch, the mortars 'would come down like hail' to keep Roffman and the rest of his unit pinned down; after every shot, the mortars would open fire again – 'The Germans were very methodical about it all.' Some time later, Julian Roffman would be put into a hospital by mortar shells and would end up in London – in time for more excitement.

Even though Germany was under almost constant air attack, and was being overrun in the east by Russian troops, the rocket launchings showed no signs of letting up. One hundred and fourteen of the missiles hit London in February, while another 90 fell short and landed in Essex. For the second month, the rockets were actually on the increase – the same number had come down last month, but January is three days longer than February. And last month, only 71 struck Essex.

Mrs Gwladys Cox thought the war news was a bit more 'cheering' – American troops had landed in the Philippines, and the Russians were still rolling into Germany – but life in London was no more encouraging than it had been since the autumn. The American, British, and Canadian troops at the Rhine were making slow progress, and it was these troops who were closest to the rocket sites. But until they could cross the Rhine, they would not be able to overrun the launch sites. And who could tell how long that might take?

Every day was punctuated by four or more jarring bangs, followed by large clouds of dark grey smoke. The number of dead and wounded was on the increase. Another 40 houses were wiped out by a V-2 on 22nd February – 19 were killed, 35 injured. Four more rockets hit London on the 23rd, producing 50 dead and about 100 injured.

A rocket's blast effects were not always felt immediately; sometimes, they took a while to make themselves known. In north west London, a missile hit and destroyed an entire row of houses in late February. A week later, the outside wall of a house, a quarter mile away from the explosion, collapsed; the entire inside of the building was exposed, like a doll's house. The inhabitants were forced to move out, and the house was later pulled down.

Frequently, victims of a rocket's blast would simply disappear, with no trace of them ever turning up. Eerie stories about the missing began circulating. The most common were in the 'haunted ruins' category – at night, the tales went, the ghost of the vanished person could be seen walking about the wreckage of their destroyed home.

Sometimes, the story was more elaborate. A teenage girl decided to take a short-cut home one evening, stepping through a vacant lot that had been a block of houses until a V-2 struck. As she made her way across the lot, another person, a woman, began walking towards her. She recognised the woman as Mrs Cusins. Mrs Cusins, a friend of the girl's mother, used to live on that block; her body was never recovered from the wreckage of her house.

Mrs Cusins came to within six feet of the girl, spoke two words, 'Stay back,' and disappeared. The girl stopped moving, more from fright than anything else. In the fading daylight, she could barely make out a large hole directly in front of her – it was either a cellar or a large crater – about ten feet deep. After a second, she turned around and ran all the way home. Her mother didn't believe her story, but the girl would never go back to that spot. Even years later, when the block had been rebuilt, she avoids walking past the place whenever she can, and refused to look at it.

'This constant harassment from the air probably prevented many a launch,' Hans van Wouw Koeleman said about the Allied fighter-bomber sweeps in and around The Hague. 'The planes kept the Germans on the move, looking for new launching sites.'

One of the main launching sites was in the Haagsche Bosch, a tree-filled park in the centre of The Hague, much like London's Hyde Park or New York's Central Park. The trees, 'tall beeches and oaks', kept the rockets hidden from enemy aircraft even when the missiles were in a vertical launching position. 'There was enough natural camouflage there to keep the Allies guessing where the next launch would be set up.'

Early in March, the rockets were on the increase again – five and six were hitting London every day instead of four – in spite of what Hans van Wouw Koeleman called 'constant harassment'. Since the fighter-bomber attacks were not doing the job, the only alternative was to launch an air raid on the Haagsche Bosch.

Allied planners were reluctant to send bombers against such a small target – the Haagsche Bosch was about a mile and a half long by a half-mile wide – situated in the middle of a populated area. Bombing raids on the liquid oxygen plants had been called off for this reason. But now the high-ranking air force officers felt that they had no choice: one sharp, precise attack might destroy a number of the elusive launch vehicles, or at least force them out of the wooded park and out into the open.

On 3rd March 56 RAF Mitchell and Boston medium bombers attacked the Haagsche Bosch; between them, the aircraft carried a total of 69 tons of bombs. Hans van Wouw Koeleman could see the planes, but couldn't tell if they were British or American. 'It was a dreary day,' he recalls, and the bombers were making their run from about 12,000 feet.

Anti-aircraft fire was murderous – 'The Germans threw ... everything but the kitchen sink,' young Hans observed. The heavy flak, along with incorrect allowance for wind, caused the bomb crews to drop their loads wide of the target. Bombs came down about 500 yards south of the target, on a section of The Hague called *Bezuidenhout*, meaning 'South of the Woods'.

Several large fires broke out, and many houses were destroyed. Hans van Wouw Koeleman estimates that hundreds of people were killed instantly, and that many more burned to death. After the All Clear sounded, Hans and the others began pulling the wounded from their houses. Civilians had to do it all themselves, since German authorities would not allow the Fire Brigade to go out; the reason given was that *die dumme Holländer mussen mal lernen was es ist* – 'the stupid Dutch have to learn what it is like'.

That night, Hans van Wouw Koeleman's house was filled with refugees from the bombed section of town – friends, relatives, and strangers. Most had left their ruined houses without taking anything along, certainly not any food. This made things very difficult for Hans' parents; the prices of food were outrageous, and the food was not always of the best quality. Hans and his family found themselves eating tulip bulbs, sugar beets, and even the leaves off trees. Fortunately, most of the unexpected guests were gone within a few days.

Both the British and American air forces learned their lesson the hard way. After this disaster, there were no more attacks on The Hague by bombers. 'Armed reconnaissance' sorties were kept up, however, and rail routes still came under constant strafing attacks by marauding fighter patrols.

Besides the rockets and trains and road traffic, there were now new targets to worry about: the Flying Bombs were back in business. A new version of the buzz bomb, made of lighter metal for longer range, appeared at the beginning of March. Three ramps for launching the new Flying Bombs were built in Western Holland, aligned on London; the new bombs could reach the British capital from that distance.

The three ramps fired only 275 Flying Bombs between them; one of the catapults was knocked out by RAF fighter-bombers within days after it became operational. Only 125 flew far enough to be picked up by the British defence network. Fighters, anti-aircraft and balloons destroyed 91. Of the 34 that got through, only 15 hit London.

These new doodlebugs were just one more slap-in-the-face that London had to endure. Occasionally, a person would see one of the black machines scuttling overhead, making their unique stuttering noise. Then the noise would stop and the plane would go into a sudden dive. A few seconds later, it hit the ground with a jarring explosion and a dense puff of smoke. The only difference between this and last summer's attack was that the Flying Bombs were now only coming over one at a time.

During the end of February, Goebbels had threatened that the attack on London would worsen. 'Goebbels kept his word,' Mrs Gwladys Cox said. 'During the past week, the bombing has got much worse again.'

Besides the rockets and Flying Bombs, Mrs Cox wrongly thought that piloted bombers were also raiding London. The incoming Flying Bombs set off the air raid sirens on 3rd March for the first time in a month and a half. '... it has been a long time since the sirens have wailed,' Mrs Cox lamented.

Julian Roffman was back in London after recovering from wounds inflicted by mortar fire in Holland. He was walking along Regent Street when 'a blast of air' rushed down the avenue, blowing out shop windows and sending Roffman diving for a doorway. He thought it was a V-2 rocket that created the blast wave but it must have been a Holland-launched Flying Bomb, since no V-2 hit anywhere near Regent Street.

Ever since those mortar attacks landed him in a hospital, Julian Roffman developed a healthy respect for blast waves – he remembers that when he was wounded, 'I felt nothing then except a blast and a giant hand pushing me aside.' Roffman bolted into a doorway to get out of the way of the oncoming wave, leaving a little space between himself and the wall 'in case the blast intensified'.

There was already a news vendor in the doorway when Roffman arrived. The little fellow was huddled on the floor and shaking, muttering, 'I can't tyke it anymore. I can't tyke it ...' Roffman did his best to calm the man, talking to him and telling him that it was all over, but then the air raid sirens started up. Even the local defences had apparently been taken by surprise; the Alert did not sound until well after the buzz bomb crashed.

Although the Russian armies were advancing into Germany from the east, the British, Canadian, and American forces in the west – the forces closest to the launch sites in Holland – were still held up at the River Rhine. The bridges across the Rhine had been destroyed by the retreating Wehrmacht, a desperate attempt to stop the Allied drive. This was not going to stop the push into Germany, but it certainly was delaying any moves. It would take quite a while before enough boats could be brought up to stage a major offensive across the Rhine.

But on 7th March an unexpected opportunity presented itself. The US 1st Army discovered that the Ludendorff Railway Bridge at the town of Remagen was still intact; the bridge was supposed to have been blown up, but the demolition charges had been shot up by artillery fire.

American troops and vehicles rushed across the bridge before the enemy had a chance to counter-attack. Within 24 hours, nearly 8,000 men were 'across the Rhine with dry feet'. By 9th March the 1st Army had established a defence perimeter three miles into

Western Germany, beating off piecemeal attacks while men and machines kept on coming across.

Since the German forces could not beat back the invading Americans, they tried to destroy the bridge. Luftwaffe bombers attacked it. So did the giant howitzer 'Karl', mounted on a railway carriage and firing shells weighing 4,400 lbs each, which broke down after only a few rounds. Also, eleven V-2 rockets were fired, most of which hit the town of Remagen.

All these attempts did not destroy the bridge, but did weaken it. On 17th March it collapsed – the vibrations caused by ten days of heavy bombardment and constant traffic had taken their toll. But by then, floating Treadway bridges had been built across the Rhine by US Army engineers; more troops and equipment kept reinforcing the bridgehead into Germany.

'OVER THE RHINE – WITH TANKS' read a London headline. It certainly was good news. But London had heard a lot of good news in the past few months, which somehow always seemed to be followed by bad. And there was still no end to the enemy attacks. On 6th March the day before the Remagen Bridge was captured, a Holland-launched Flying Bomb hit a power station in Barking, Essex – the station was blown up, and surrounding property suffered severe damage.

Two days later, on the morning of 8th March, Leonard Lincoln was driving a small van back to its garage after making a unique delivery. Lincoln was employed by a large bank in the City of London, and had just dropped off one and one quarter million pounds in Bank of England notes. He and two other staff members had completed their errand and were just passing Smithfield Market, at 11 a.m., when they heard 'a terrific explosion'.

Lincoln immediately stopped the van; at the same instant, the fuel tank exploded, enveloping the vehicle in flames. He managed to stagger away from the van despite a broken ankle and badly burned face and hands. The other two men escaped without a scratch.

During the Middle Ages, Smithfield was the site of many public executions. In the nineteenth century, during excavations for fitting sewer pipes, a pile of blackened stones and human bones were discovered; these were the remains of religious martyrs, burned alive during the reign of Mary Tudor three hundred years before. Since the 1860s, the northern part of this district had been occupied by the Central Markets, one of London's leading meat and provisions distributors.

A V-2 rocket had hit the north-western corner of the long, narrow market complex, about 30 yards from Leonard Lincoln's van. The market had just received a large shipment of fish that morning; a long queue was waiting to buy the unrationed fish when the rocket impacted and exploded.

The Central Markets Building itself was a solidly-built, three-storey structure, with outer walls of brick and masonry and an inside structure of rusting ironwork. When staff worker Ron Fowler, on the ground floor, heard what sounded like a distant explosion, he breathed a sigh of relief that the blast was far off. Then his vision was blocked by a heavy black fog – the years of dust and dirt cascading down from the rafters. Without any kind of warning, bricks and chunks of concrete next began falling all around him.

Ron Fowler remained frozen underneath an overhead meat rail, which protected him from the falling upper works. The 'fog' slowly cleared, and he could see daylight above where there should have been two upper floors.

His glasses had been blown off, and he could feel a heavy weight pulling him down. His first thought was that he had been badly injured, that he had lost a limb. When he looked, however, Fowler found two large sides of meat from the overhead rail hooked to his overalls.

After shedding the hunks of meat, Fowler headed out of the wrecked building 'over mountains of debris', without stopping to look for his glasses. Along with two fellow workers, he stopped to survey the wreckage and noted that a fire had broken out. After a few minutes, he realised that he was standing on something soft; Fowler looked at his feet and found a body lying face down. He stumbled away in complete shock.

Those who were close to the explosion cannot remember hearing a 'boom' at all, just the force of powerful blast waves pushing against them. A civilian who was coming up from an Underground station at the moment of impact first heard a 'ripping sound' that

The Smithfield Market Rocket Incident: '... at the same instant, the fueltank exploded, enveloping the vehicle in flames.' Members of the London Fire Brigade hose down a blasted-out van a short time after the rocket hit.

The Smithfield Market Rocket Incident: 'A V-2 rocket had hit the north-western corner of the long, narrow market complex ...' After the wreckage was cleared away, an inside wall of the now roofless market section stares blankly down at observers.

kept getting louder. This was followed by 'a wooshing rush of air –
as if a giant were loudly drawing in his breath.'

A third of a mile south of the Market at St Paul's Cathedral, an
American officer was on a sightseeing tour. He felt 'a strong
concussion', then saw smoke rising from Smithfield. The tour guide
later told everybody what happened.

An official police report states that buildings within a quarter-
mile radius of the blast were rendered unsafe, every structure on 29
adjoining streets was damaged. The casualty count totalled 115
dead, 123 injured. Police dogs were brought in to search the rubble
for victims. Several days later, the Rescue Squad was still digging.

By afternoon on 8th March the site that had been Ron Fowler's
shop was occupied by a heavy crane for clearing away debris. One
of Ron Fowler's friends, an 18-year-old boy who was about to be
called up for the services, was missing until next day. On 9th
March his body was found inside one of the market complex's
demolished rooms, two storeys off the ground.

Leonard Lincoln fell into 'a space about 30 feet deep' after
hobbling away from his burned-out van. He was found after only a
short while and taken to nearby St Bartholomew's Hospital. At 'St
Bart's' Lincoln's fractured ankle was wrapped in a heavy plaster
cast; the doctors on duty in the ward called him 'The man with a
million'.

Although the Smithfield Market incident stands out as one of the
worst, it was far from the last rocket explosion to happen in
London. Every day, usually during the morning hours, from four to
six explosions would shatter the cool March greyness. And on 15th
March a Holland-launched Flying Bomb hit an ordinance depot in
London and 'half demolished' it, according to the official report.

On the same day, 15th March, the US 3rd and 7th armies
launched a second drive into Germany. The Wehrmacht was
fighting back, but everybody knew that the war would not last
much longer. Supply routes into Holland remained open, however,
and the V-2 launches against London went on, as fierce as ever.

'Although we realise it is Hitler's last fling, it is nevertheless very
unpleasant,' commented Mrs Gwladys Cox. '... we are all utterly
weary and feel we do not deserve this flare-up, even if it is the
finale.' Another Londoner put it more succinctly: 'No one wants to

General Walter Dornberger (left) and Wernher von Braun, arm in cast from an auto accident, after surrendering to American forces in 1945.

be killed by the last bullet.'

If the people in London knew the war was ending, the launch crews in Holland knew it also. Toward the middle of March, in one last burst of energy, the rocket batteries launched 13 or more V-2s per day. Volume was not matched by accuracy, however. Many of the shots went well astray; the daily average hitting London remained at five rockets.

The fears of the rocket crews were well founded. General George Patton opened a second bridgehead across the Rhine on 23rd March, north of the crossing at Remagen. Almost immediately, this new offensive began blocking supply routes to the launch sites, and the rate of rockets being fired began to slacken.

But the shots did continue. William Johnson, a pupil at Tottenham Grammar School in North London, had gone to the library during lunch break. He heard no explosion to indicate that a missile had arrived, but there was a 'sudden rush of air' and the room was filled with dust. Luckily, casualties and damage to the school were both light, although at least one boy died when blast waves threw him against a wall, crushing his skull.

On 27th March all rocket units were ordered to withdraw from Holland into Germany; General Patton's troops were threatening to cut them off. One of the parting shots fired by the launching units destroyed a block of flats in Stepney, East London. The missile scored a direct hit, collapsing the building and badly damaging another nearby block. After all the bodies had been dug out, several days later, the death toll was placed at 134, with 49 injured.

About two hours later, the last V-2 to hit Britain came down on Orpington, Kent, about 20 miles south-east of London.

The rocket attack was over, but the Flying Bombs still had a few more days left. One of the pilotless planes landed on London on 27th March, three hit on the 28th, and the last crashed into a small town north of London on the morning of 29th March. After 29th March, there were no more air raid Alerts in London or anywhere in Great Britain, over four and a half years after the first sirens during the summer of 1940.

Afterwards, with the benefit of hindsight, some self-proclaimed 'experts' would claim that the pilotless planes and the long-range guided missiles were a failure. As evidence, all the things that the weapons did not do were pointed out – they did not win the war for Germany; they were used too late to stop the D-Day landings. But the things that the secret weapons did accomplish far outweigh any negative remarks against them.

During the Flying Bomb assault, from mid-June to early September 1944, 2,419 of the pilotless aircraft crash-dived into London. Rail and transportation networks were seriously disrupted. War production fell off. Damages inflicted, including lost factory production, totalled £48m – about $150 million. Allied casualties came to over 8,000, including 2,000 airmen. German casualties: 185 killed.

Between 8th September 1944 and 27th March 1945, 517 V-2 rockets struck London, with another 378 falling short of their target and impacting in Essex. Throughout southern England, a grand total of 1,054 came down. In London alone over 2,700 civilians were dead from the rockets. Industry suffered considerable loss and morale, especially in London, was badly shaken. German casualties: 51 dead, 117 wounded.

The war still had six weeks to run, until 8th May 1945. Just before the formal surrender, Wernher von Braun and General Walter Dornberger would give themselves up to American forces, along with most of Germany's rocket scientists.

General Dornberger was held as a prisoner of war, and was supposed to have stood trial for attacks on London and Antwerp. But the trial never took place. Dornberger came to live in the United States in the late 1940s. Wernher von Braun also came to the US, and became one of the leading figures in the American space programme in the 1950s and 1960s.

But for London, the war came to an end with the last Flying Bomb on 29th March; from then on, the fighting existed only on the radio and in the newspapers. Nobody realised that the rockets and Flying Bombs were finished, but the quiet came as a welcome relief, especially after the fury of the last few weeks. On 1st April 1945 a woman made this entry in her diary: 'No sirens, no explosions for three whole days – Peace, it's wonderful.'

A Note on Sources

This book is based chiefly upon the recollections of the many people who were kind enough to respond to my request for information and who are listed at the beginning of the text. Among the printed sources which supplied background information are: *The Gunner*, an article in which by General Frederick Pile shed much light on anti-aircraft activities against the Flying Bomb; London editions of *Stars and Stripes* and the *ARP and NFS News* gave personal angles on the war with the German secret weapons; *Crusade in Europe* by Dwight D. Eisenhower (Doubleday 1948) gave an excellent account of the war in Europe; Walter Dornberger's *V-2* (Hurst & Blacket, 1954) was a fascinating personal account of the development of the long-range rocket. *The Mare's Nest* by David Irving (William Kimber, 1964) I referred to time and again for its detailed technical information on the V-Weapons, especially the V-2. *The Year of the Buzz Bomb* by Richard B. Baker (Exposition Press 1952) told of life in London during the German secret weapons' attack, and was a highly informative journal.

INDEX

Index

About the author:

David Johnson interviewed eyewitnesses on both sides of the Atlantic while researching *V-1/V-2,* and he was given access to previously classified documents and photographs. Mr. Johnson is also the author of *The London Blitz.* He lives in Union, New Jersey.